I Could Write a Book!

A Scottish-Australian Adventure

I Could Write a Book!
A Scottish-Australian Adventure

JOY SNELLING

Text Nick Hagan, on behalf of StoryTerrace

Design Grade Design and Adeline Media, London

Copyright © Joy Snelling

CONTENTS

FOREWORD

This book is dedicated to the three nutters I am so lucky to call my sons and daughter – Lewis, Innis and Hazel – and also to my son-in-law, Conor, who has become a big part of our family. It's also dedicated to Granny, whose cheeky smile we'll never forget, and Derek, a beloved friend who left us far too soon. We'll think of you whenever we see those £1 bunches of daffodils!

I also have to mention my good friend Les: if it wasn't for her I wouldn't have even thought of looking for someone to write my book, and I would never have met Nick Hagan, my ghostwriter, who I hope will become a lifelong friend!

And last but not least, my best friend, who has been by my side through thick and thin for the last 37 years, my darling husband Andy. Without you, none of this would ever have happened.

TOWARDS THE RED CENTRE

(21st to 28th May 2018)

As we turn out of Perth and onto State Route 94, the sat nav smoothly announces its next instruction.

"Stay on for 524 kilometres."

I glance across to the driver's seat at Andy. He looks back.

"Well. Looks like we won't be needing directions for a while..."

As it turns out, we won't be needing them at all. There's only one road out from here: the road through nowhere. And our little car, practically groaning from the strain of all our bags, is about to take it. For six days on the trot.

It's not yet seven o'clock in the morning, but in the backseat Barney the dog is already panting a little. It's going to be a hot one – at least by our standards. Even though it's technically late Autumn here. That certainly takes a bit of getting used to.

In fact, I can already tell that Australia in general is going to take a bit of getting used to. The weather, the people, the culture: it all feels a bit back-to-front compared to home. But this is it. Our big Aussie adventure – the start of a new life down under. Now, it's time to move on to the next chapter.

So let's go. We turn the sat nav off, turn the stereo up and turn onto the highway, full of uncertainty and excitement, to start the journey of our lifetimes.

Two Days Later

What the hell are we doing here?

They call it the Nullarbor plain. It means 'no trees' – and they're not kidding, I'll tell you. For miles in every direction, as far as the eye can see, the land is flat and dusty, with a red-brown tint. The road seems never-ending. It cuts through the desert, straight as an arrow, to disappear as a dot on the horizon. The occasional dead kangaroo alongside the road breaks up the monotony, but for hours at a time there's just dust, road, sky... that's it.

It took a little over two days of driving from Perth to get to the Nullarbor – and we still have four to go. I've never seen such a desolate place in my life, and again I can't help but wonder what the hell we're doing out here, in the middle of all this nothing. Two lost Scots, in the middle of Australia! It's all a bit disorientating, a bit surreal. There are moments when I have to remind myself that there's a destination at the end of it.

But then, we've been waiting for this for, what... five years, give or take? Ever since Lewis, Hazel and Innis moved away, the idea of following them to Australia has been brewing.

And I'd be lying if I said it wasn't exciting. One of the most exciting things we've ever done, by far. We spend each day chatting, arguing over what to listen to on the stereo (Robbie Williams is currently winning) and just taking in this vast expanse of wilderness all around us.

It's a timings game, driving the Nullarbor. There's a string of petrol stations (known as 'servos' to the Aussies) and a handful of roadhouses dotted along the way. They're few and far between as you'd expect, so you have to stop whenever you see one. You can't get blasé about water or fuel out here.

So far, we've managed to get it right – there's been no need to unload the swag from the luggage and spend a night by the roadside, thank god. There's no way to drive the Nullarbor plain by night – too much risk of a stray roo or emu causing an accident. Then you'd really be screwed, stuck in the middle of nowhere with a broken car and no Wi-Fi! Thankfully, we've timed our travel well enough to stay at a roadhouse each night instead.

Come to think of it, timing is really the reason we're here, too, speaking more generally. As we said to each other back in Inverness, it's now or never. If we don't give this adventure a try now, we'll miss our chance. So we took the plunge. And now we're here, on the road, embracing the spirit of adventure! Whatever's over the horizon, in the red centre, waiting for us in Alice Springs – we're ready to meet it.

1

AN ADVENTUROUS FAMILY

I think it was all the holidays that started it.

As the kids were growing up, we began going on these big group getaways with our neighbours, Maurice, Doreen and their daughter Marina. I can still remember the first time they suggested it.

"Hey, we should all go on holiday together."

"Oh, I dunno... all eight of us together?"

I was a bit unsure; it sounded like a logistical nightmare, to be honest. But we're such good friends with them that the idea sunk in pretty fast. The first holiday we ever had together was at Center Parcs, sharing a big villa. It was so much fun we did it again the next year, this time for five days, with villas next door to each other – the three of them and the five of us. Another fantastic break – and after that, we all ventured on our first holiday abroad, to Crete. That was it. Travelling had now become a tradition. Every year, we'd go away together – usually to Turkey, or to Cyprus. There are so many great memories from those trips, and they definitely made an impression on the kids. We must have gone to Turkey about four or five years on the trot, to the point where the kids actually started complaining about it!

"Are we going to bloody Turkey again?"

"Yes, and you're bloody lucky to be getting any holiday!"

The last one Lewis came on, when he was 15, we even hopped

over from Cyprus to Egypt. A holiday within a holiday! Hazel was 13, Innis 11. It only cost £500 for the five of us – we couldn't pass up an opportunity like that. Egypt was just amazing.

Lewis was starting to get a bit tired of the family trips by then, in full teenager mode. But I remember how exciting it was for Innis. He was a little bugger back then, always getting me into bother. I remember a time in Egypt, when we were walking through a street market together, just me and him. He saw a watch he liked, and we went to buy it off the street seller. It was a knock off – a total piece of crap. But Innis really wanted it, so we tried to barter with the salesman. To our surprise he wanted an absolute bomb for it, a ridiculous price. He wouldn't budge. I was ready to walk away, but Innis was just desperate for the watch. So I just went, "You'll take this!" I threw down some money and we walked briskly away, watch still in hand.

Behind us, he starts shouting, "Come back, you're stealing!"

So we ran! We dashed through the streets all the way back to the ship we were staying on. My heart was going mad. He shouted after us, calling us thieves. I wasn't having it.

"You've got your money, it's a crap watch anyway!"

Sure enough, it broke about a week after we got home.

Was it these trips that led to our family's Aussie saga? It's hard to say really, but I certainly think it had something to do with it. After Lewis stopped coming on holiday, there were seven of us taking the annual trip. Next Hazel went off to uni – six; Innis too – five; and at last Marina stopped joining, leaving just the parents. That didn't stop us enjoying ourselves, mind you. We carried on visiting Egypt, and had some wonderful times in Sharm and along the Nile.

But it wasn't that long before the kids got the travel bug again – and Australia and the Far East suddenly became a fixture for our family. It started in December 2009, when Lewis went down under for the first time. He came back for my 50th birthday the following summer, and wouldn't stop talking about moving.

"I'm going to Australia," he'd announce.

Hazel and Innis either didn't believe him, or didn't want to.

"No you're not! I *bet* you won't."

The wheels were turning. That year Lewis's friend Debbie went over to Oz herself, in the hope of getting sponsored to stay there by the hairdressers she worked for. She invited Lewis to go over with her, so suddenly he had his chance to go back. Sadly Debbie didn't get sponsored in the end and came back to Scotland, but Lewis decided to stay. It's funny how these things work out.

Fast forward two years and Hazel has wrapped up her education, completing her Master's in chemistry. She started looking for teaching work, and went to interview for a secondary school, but despite her best efforts it was hard to find a position. The nearest town is Inverness – it's not like we've got Edinburgh or Glasgow right on our doorstep. It went on like that for a few months, until one day she came downstairs and said, "Look, I'm just going to go to Australia to see Lewis. I can't get any work here."

So it was time to see Hazel off too. She graduated from Strathclyde University on a Friday in July, so we went down for the ceremony, and the day after we drove her to the airport. She had swapped her graduation gowns for a backpacker's get-up: one big backpack on her back, a little one on the front and her handbag! And off she went.

None of this was a huge surprise, because we've always been an adventurous family. Lewis had been talking about it for a while, and then he took the plunge. It wasn't Hazel's first big adventure, either. At school she had gone on trips to France, the Gambia, Botswana. For her fourth year at uni she had lived in Germany, to work on a placement with Bayer, the big pharmaceutical company. All we ever did was say cheerio to each other, so going to Oz came pretty naturally.

The way Andy and I see it, our kids have got their own lives. We didn't bring them up to hang onto our apron strings – we brought them up to be the independent people that they are today. We're very proud of that.

They never ask for money from us. We offered to help Lewis when he was going through a tough time trying to leave a bad relationship. He said, "No, I'm not taking your money. You can't afford it." They're like that. Innis won't give me his bank details to put money into his account for his birthday! That's the kind of kids they are – strong and self-sufficient.

I know people who have said to their kids: "You can't leave me. You can't go abroad." A former friend turned around and said to me, "What did you and Andy do wrong?" I said, "We didn't do anything wrong. We brought them up to be independent." Do you want to be in your 70s or 80s and your kids are still at home, looking after you? I don't want that, for me or them.

Innis, Hazel and Lewis have travelled so far, and lived in so many places abroad. And I think it all goes back to Center Parcs! It's quite probably all because Andy and I set them out on that road when we took them on holiday with our friends and neighbours.

The other thing that's important to remember is that there were so many good memories at home, too.

One thing we used to do together as a family, which I will always think of fondly, was going to visit my mum in Fort Augustus. It's only about an hour's drive from Inverness, and about once a month we would go over for the Sunday. It was always a highlight, going to see Granny. She'd cook us up a big pot of stew, her speciality. Me and Hazel would tuck into that, and because Andy's a vegetarian he and Lewis would order in a huge pizza from Bici's in Inverness. My mum would always have a massive bag of sweets for the kids, too – you should have seen the size of it! Kinder Eggs will always remind me of her.

It goes to show it's not always the most far-flung or exotic moments in life that stay with you. We all had that adventurous spirit, but those Sundays at Granny's were a really special treat too. Some of the best memories are made at home.

Myself and my mum

Andy and my mum

Lewis and Granny

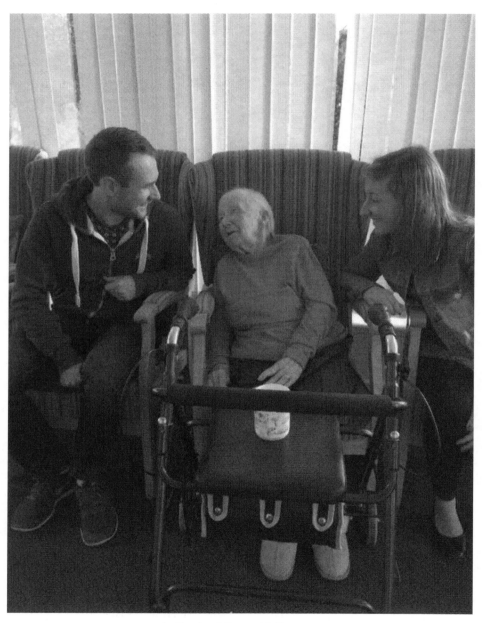

Hazel and Conor with Granny

Innis with Granny

2

SHOULD WE STAY OR SHOULD WE GO?

(November 2012 to April 2017)

My first impression of Australia was: *it's really bloody hot.*

And that's in spite of the Christmas trees. Yes, it was Christmastime when Andy and I first visited, coming up to the end of 2012. Our flight landed late in the evening, and Hazel and Lewis were there to meet us at the airport.

Everyone was shattered that first night, so we had a brief reunion and then just retired to the hotel. Andy and I were up again by about 4am the next morning though; your body clock goes haywire when you've been through so many time zones. It was certainly the longest flight either of us have ever been on – and Andy truly hates flying. But suddenly, there we were, awake at stupid o'clock in the morning in the Land Down Under. I made a call to Andy's uncle Jeff, who also lives in Australia. After that, we got up and went for a wander around the town. The shops weren't open yet, but already the sun was shining brightly. We walked down the streets, and in every window a Christmas tree sat twinkling.

I remember thinking, I am gonna love this.

A bit later on, at a more reasonable hour, we met the kids for breakfast, followed by a tour of Perth. The feeling of excitement only intensified. There was so much to see, so many shops, sights and landmarks. It was amazing. It just seemed like such a lovely place.

Then it was time for Lewis to drive us out to where he lived. We hadn't quite appreciated the distance. As we got in the car, Lewis turned and said, "Take one last look, Mum, because you're not gonna see Perth again for another three weeks!"

"Eh? What do you mean?"

"Where we live – well, it's not like this. You'll see."

What to make of that? Well, I needn't have worried. Three and a half hours later we were in Dunsborough, and while I had loved the look of Perth, this place was, as Lewis had promised, Heaven on Earth. A different sort of place altogether, a beautiful little seaside town, even smaller than Nairn, where Andy's mum Sally lives back in Scotland. Right next to the Indian Ocean, and dotted with all these beautiful little beaches. You don't just say, "Let's go to the beach," in Dunsborough. You say, "Let's go to Smith's Beach," or, "Let's go to Eagle Bay, or Yallingup." The coastline is just dotted with wonderful little sandy coves.

It was hard not to fall in love with the place. For three weeks we committed to unwinding, spending quality time together as a family and soaking up the atmosphere of the coast. Of course, the seed of an idea was planted, too. Once we'd had a taste, we couldn't help but start thinking about what it might be like to sell up back home, to chuck it all in and move out to paradise, near to the kids again. You couldn't help but dream of it, being somewhere like this.

Hazel and I would talk about it, weighing up the pros and cons.

"Mum, you'll never live in Dunsborough. You'll miss the shops too much."

"You know, there's more to life than Marks and Spencer, Hazel. It's all online now anyway..."

After three weeks we were back in Inverness again, already missing Lewis and Hazel and the coast like crazy. But it wasn't just the memories from Dunsborough we had brought back – the idea that, just maybe, we could make our own life in Australia had also taken root.

More trips would follow. The next year, all the kids came home for Christmas, and then in 2014 and 2015 Andy and I went back to see them in Oz in turn. Each time we would see a bit more of Western Australia, appreciating its charm, and the thought got a bit stronger in turn: We could live here.

The truth was, Andy and I weren't getting any younger. We both wanted to be near the kids again. We missed them. But it wasn't a quick decision, either. By 2015 I was 55, and the idea of emigrating had become more than just pie in the sky. We were really considering it now, talking about the practicalities of a move in depth.

This is where our different styles of personality come into view. Andy, as ever, was very decisive, positive, clear-eyed.

"Let's just do it!" he declared. Ready to go in a heartbeat.

But I, being me, needed some time to swither and dither about it.

"It's not just a case of 'let's do it', Andy. We'd be selling up!"

And I was right to put the brakes on a bit. If we did take the plunge, it would be a big deal.

The kids could see both sides of it. Lewis and Hazel, for their part, were quite sanguine, sensible about it.

"Well, we'd love to have you both. But if you sell up, that's it. You've got no home. All your money's invested, and you'll be taking that out and using it up."

Well, if we were stupid that could happen, sure. The risk was obviously there – but would there be more risk in us not going?

"I don't know, Andy. I really just don't know if we can do this."

"I tell you, if we don't do it now we'll never do it. We might live to regret it."

Wasn't that the whole thing in a nutshell? We were in our 50s, our kids had left home, I was sick to death of my job at the doctor's surgery. We both had an urge for something fresh, some kind of adventure. It was calling to us.

So gradually, my perspective started to change. You know, life is short. I'm a great believer that what is meant to be is meant to be. It was our moment to do this! I may swither and dither, but when my mind's made up there's no turning back. It was the start of 2016, and we had come to our decision. We were going to Australia.

Soon after, I officially left my job at the doctor's surgery. This would be the year of preparation, and there was much to do before we could head off into the sunset. Perhaps most important, the house would need to be sold. We put it on the market and began wrapping up everything else.

It was a strange and exciting time; the thought that we might really be leaving, and not coming back, took a while to sink in. Lewis and Hazel both came back to Scotland to go to friends' weddings, so we saw them for a bit. But really, 2016 was just a blur of activity, trying to get everything in order so we could make a real go of Australia.

Summer came, and Hazel and her partner Conor suggested we join them in Rome for my birthday, as a treat. Well, why not – what a great way to kick off our life-changing decision! We headed over, and when we met them in the airport Hazel had a surprise for us. She held up her hand, showing a big ring on her finger.

"We got engaged!"

I peered at her hand.

"No you didn't. That ring's on the wrong finger."

"Conor! I told you she'd say that!"

They had gotten the measurement wrong.

That was a great trip – we were celebrating both Hazel and Conor's engagement and my birthday, so you can imagine how many glasses

were raised. Every five minutes it was, "Cheers to the engagement!
"Happy Birthday!"

I had been dreading our leaving do. I just find goodbyes really hard.
As I explained to my friends, I couldn't have a party one week and fly
off to Australia the next. I'd be too upset.

The only option was to leave a longer gap. So we hosted the party
between Christmas and New Year 2016. The house was up for sale,
and it seemed certain we would be flying off to Australia the following
year. It was an open house party, and we were surprised at how many
of our friends turned up, and at the mixture; I was really struck, on
the brink of saying goodbye, by how varied a spectrum of friends
we have. We know people from all walks of life, from tradesmen to
professionals like doctors, scientists, public defenders. The Christmas
decorations were still up, and I was reminded of the parties we had
had at Christmases past; really informal affairs at which everyone was
welcome and people stayed to enjoy themselves for hours. It was the
same that night. Things didn't wrap up until 4am, and it just felt special
to have so many friends together in one space like that. It's also just
as wonderful to think that many of the friends who said goodbye to
us then were also there to welcome us back from Alice two years later.

Then, all of a sudden, it was 2017: the year of Australia!

With all that time to plan and prepare, our ambitions had also
developed a bit. Andy and I have always loved roaming around,
visiting new places – the freedom that it brings. So, after the house sold
in February, we got ourselves a camper van. It was just a no-brainer:
let's explore the British Isles as a warm-up before we head out to Oz.
Andy had finished his job and packed his business up. We sold the
house in April, and all our stuff was emptied out and put into storage.
We were ready to hit the road.

But not before one last visit from our very good friends, Den and

Jackie. We still had the house for one last weekend before Sue – the new owner, who is now also a good friend – moved in. We've been spending time with Den and Jackie for years. We always have such a laugh with each other. What I didn't mention on this occasion was that, with all our stuff in storage, we'd all be sleeping in the camper – including our guests. It felt like we were at a festival, but in our back garden! We had a picnic table and chairs, so we could eat dinner outside. So much fun.

Then, at last, it really was time to hit the road.

It was great – genuinely such a lovely way to start our adventure of a lifetime. We went all around the UK, all the way down to Land's End, as far as we could go. We loved every minute of it.

For the first leg we went up to Culloden, the campsite at the famous battlefield. Andy was still doing a bit of work at the college, so he would go off there during the day in the car, leaving me in the camper van with Barney and our two cats. It was April, and one day I looked up to see it had started to snow! It felt like a bad omen. There I was, stuck in the camper van with the heating on, in April, because it was so freezing! I started thinking to myself, What the hell have we done?

But maybe I'm more adaptable than I give myself credit for. By the time Andy came home early in the afternoon, the camper had warmed up and was all lovely and cosy. We had dinner and wine together, watching the snow fall down outside.

I said, "I think we're going to like this."

He said, "I think so too."

3

NEW HORIZONS – AND A SAD GOODBYE

(Summer 2017)

ow the hell are we all going to fit in that?

As I've mentioned, Andy is usually the one who struggles with flying. But today I have a strong feeling that I will too

First, I've never been in a helicopter before – even the sight of the things outside the airport reception makes me feel queasy. They don't look very big, or very secure. In fact, if I'm honest, they're bloody tiny.

And so is the pilot. She looks about 12, a wee slip of a thing. I always say Hazel looks much younger than she actually is, but compared to this lassie she's positively ancient. She honestly looks like a teenager on holiday.

At a glance, it's an accident waiting to happen. But despite our reservations, we all climb aboard the copters – one for family, one for Lewis's friends – and strap in. The blades begin to whir, and before we know it we're swallowed up by the roar of the machine. It might be small, but clearly it's powerful! It's enough to set my heart racing. We've all got those big chunky headphones on so we can speak and hear each other over the din.

When we lift off, my heart is in my mouth. The nose dips down as the copter rises, and we're away! Below us, the rocky, golden-brown desert extends in all directions – real Wild West country, just like in the movies. It's an absolute adrenaline rush. I love it!

Next to me though, Andy is just a bit nervous. His complexion has dropped a few shades.

"How young is she?" he asks through his headphone mic.

I turn to our pilot.

"How old are you?"

"Oh, I'm 22," she says casually. She explains that she got her licence fairly recently.

Looking back at Andy, I see one train of thought expressed in his face: This is the end. We're not going to make it to the Hoover Dam, let alone Australia.

Thankfully, our pilot is more competent than we give her credit for. Pretty soon Vegas is behind us and we're soaring across the desert – and what an epic sight to behold.

We're all starting to relax a bit more, even Andy. The sheer splendour of the landscape below is just captivating.

But then, quite suddenly, the helicopter *drops*.

"Oh *shit*!" yells Andy. He's starting to panic – this, after all, is his worst nightmare.

A second later, as quickly as it dipped, the copter levels out once more. All returns to normal, as much as this sort of thing can be thought of as normal.

"Ah sorry – we hit an air pocket there. Shoulda told you about the dip," our pilot offers.

Poor Andy. If he was pale before, he's now positively ghost-like.

It was June 2017, and we had flown out to Nevada – to Las Vegas no less – to crash our Lewis's 30th birthday party. After two months on the road in the camper, Andy and I had hopped onto a plane and jetted over the Atlantic, and over the continent, to surprise our boy. This time, it hadn't been one of the kids dropping a shock on us, like Hazel with her engagement; it had instead been the two of us, stepping out around a corner in the hotel lobby when Lewis walked in. I'll never forget the look on his face.

"What the f*** are you two doing here?!"

It was a brilliant moment – so exciting to see him again, out in Vegas. He was really happy to see us too. But in actual fact we had decided to come for another reason, besides his birthday.

We sat down at the bar for a drink, and that was our chance to explain. "Well," I said. "You know Granny's not well. She's not going to get better either. We don't know how long she's got left. But we know she'd like you to be spoiled on your birthday."

Truthfully, coming to Vegas had been a really hard choice – because my mum was dying. Her nursing home in Inverness had been in regular contact with us while we were travelling around the UK to tell us as much. At one point they gave her 48 hours, which was completely wrong. But we drove back up to see her again, of course, and it was certainly true that she was getting weaker. She was only drinking small sips of fluid, and hardly eating. It was hard seeing her like that, but nonetheless I knew she wasn't dying at first glance. Not yet.

We spoke to the home manager at length about what we should do. The trip out to Vegas for Lewis's birthday had been on the cards for a while – but if my poor mum really was getting ready to die, that complicated things. I had my hunch that she wasn't, but there was no way to be absolutely sure.

The manager was very understanding.

"You should just go. There's no point sitting around and waiting here. If she dies while you're away, we have facilities at the funeral home. Go and enjoy yourselves as best you can."

She was right. We knew Granny would want us all to be together on Lewis's 30th. It was that simple. So we went.

Even though Granny was on our mind, we had a wonderful time

in the States. It was like a celebration on her behalf. The helicopter ride ended with a picnic at the Grand Canyon, which was absolutely breath-taking. We landed, took photos and had a wee glass of bubbly, looking out at the incredible scenery, all that vast wilderness. After, we flew over the Hoover Dam, arriving back in Vegas at night-time and flying over the strip. That was a highlight, a moment I'll never forget. It felt like we were flying quite low, quite close to the ground, and all the lights were flashing, suspended around us – it was just magical. If you don't do these things one day, when will you?

Andy and I found ourselves split on Vegas – he couldn't stand the fakeness, how glitzy and American the whole thing was. I, on the other hand, found it all to be quite the novelty. It was fast-moving, it was noise, it was bright lights. It felt like one big theme park, with all these crazy, entertaining features.

We stayed at the Aria Hotel, which was typically plush and larger-than-life. It had a train that took you between buildings – very Vegas. You walked into reception, and the place was just HUGE. Turn a corner and you're right in the thick of it – endless rows of fruit machines, tables and other games. There were no clocks on any of the walls, so you lost track of time pretty quickly. And these machines were never switched off, they were going 24/7 and there was always somebody playing. They took credit card, for God's sake!

"You're not gambling," Andy said sternly. But we both knew we would; we agreed on a stake of $50, no more. We did the roulette and actually won something, before swiftly losing it again. Then, as we had promised ourselves, we stopped. It's a slippery slope. If I had loads of money I'd love to just go and sit there for a few hours, chipping away at it. But we knew we had to be smart and step away, otherwise we could kiss Australia goodbye!

That's America for you, after all – it's boom or bust, winner or loser. The point was made in a different way by a waitress we met in the hotel restaurant. She must have been in her late 50s or early 60s, by my estimate. She told us she had to keep working, because it was so expensive to live in the Las Vegas area. She travelled in every day.

Being Scottish, we found the tipping a bit tricky. Tips are a big deal in the States – you get a server for your table who relies on them, and they're expecting tips as well as their salary. But it got to the stage where we were like, "Nah, we're Scottish. You're getting nothing from us!"

Our server also told us that things used to be better when the mafia ran Vegas, which was eye-opening. Apparently the bills weren't as high, and everything ran fine. It was only when it started getting more commercialised that things got crazy expensive.

We spent five days in the land of the casinos – about all the time we could endure, honestly. Then the next leg of the trip began. Lewis drove a Mustang as part of his birthday present, and we headed to San Diego for Independence Day. We even went down over the border, into Mexico. That was scary as hell, having to get out of the car and walk across as they did the traffic check. Security and guns everywhere; a very tense atmosphere. Well worth it, though – once we got into Mexico we hired a minibus and went for a little explore. We stayed at a lovely place for one night, then headed back to the States the following day, to Palm Springs. All I can really remember about that place was the *heat*. It was unbelievable – I've never experienced anything like it. It must have been 50 degrees, so hot it just took your breath away. The apartment we were staying in had a lovely swimming pool, and Lewis and his pals were eating pizza in it.

"Are you coming in, Mum?"

"No. I'm going to sit here and melt in this chair."

What an adventure. All this, and we weren't even in Australia yet.

From Vegas back to Scotland. Granny had held on, as I had expected – there had been no update from the home. As for us, we were zombies on our arrival back to Scotland. If you've ever flown west to east, you'll know it can really rattle your body clock. By the time we got back to Inverness we were horribly jetlagged, and decided to turn our phones off for a few days to recover. When we turned them back on again, it had happened. We had a few missed calls. Granny had passed. It was 12th July.

How in God's name had she held on so long? The home had originally been in touch with us at the end of May, giving her 48 hours. In the end she had died nearly two months later.

You do not appreciate what you have, until you don't. You fall out with your mum; my kids fall out with me. It happens all the time. My mum had all these little sayings. "Oh well, one day I won't be here." And although I knew she was gonna pass away at some point, when she actually did... it's very hard to explain to somebody how you feel.

Andy was the first to find out, and when he told me she had passed it just felt so final. I told myself that she had really died weeks ago – she had been bedridden, she was sleeping all the time. We were all prepared for it, so there was no big shock. But still, there's the moment when you actually get the news, when you hear the words: "She's gone." The realisation that I'd never see her again. That was hard to process.

All the kids came home for the funeral. Lewis had barely landed in Australia when he had to board another flight back to Scotland. Innis flew over from Germany, and Hazel swithered and dithered for a while, not wanting to fly alone, then decided she would.

Granny's funeral was held at Fort Augustus, right by the shores of Loch Ness. Both she and I had been brought up there. It was a proper Highland funeral, and I was overcome by the sheer number of friends who came. They all knew my mum – even their kids did. Her name was Betty, but everyone just called her Granny. I couldn't help but imagine how chuffed she would have been as well. For an old lady who had been living away from the village for some years it was quite a turn out. She was a right busybody; she would have been looking at all the people in attendance with great curiosity, asking, "Who's that one now? Who's that?"

It was a really good send off. Because we had all known since the start of June that she was passing, we had already had most of our tears. Which meant the funeral felt like more of a celebration of her life. Of course, I was feeling sad. But there were so many memories to share.

Granny had always been one for doom and gloom, which added a bit of humour to things when the minister spoke about it. She had all her phrases: "Sure as death" was a well-worn favourite. At the end of every Christmas she would say, with a sigh, "If we're spared till next year maybe we'll see another Christmas."

We were always like, "What? You'll see more of them than we bloody will!"

She was a character, my mum. Good craic. We buried her with a half-bottle of whisky and a pack of playing cards – she was a card shark after all, she taught all the kids how to play. She'll be up in Heaven with her cards and her bottle, no doubt, asking, "Who's up for a game?"

And she would have loved all the male attention she got. She had always wanted Lewis to have the head cord at her funeral, with Innis second and Andy third. She'd have been so happy to see all those men lowering her into the ground! Lewis threw a bouquet of flowers into the grave right at the end. It was a very beautiful moment.

What a whirlwind of a summer it had been. When I think back on it now, I'm sincerely glad that we made the call to be with Lewis for his 30th – it really is what Granny would have wanted. She was an easygoing soul who just fitted in, and never wanted to ruin anything for anybody. In a way, we all came together in Vegas for her, and once more for her send off. No doubt she'll be remembered at all sorts of future family gatherings, too. That cheeky smile was now just a memory – but a memory we'd never forget.

It was now over six months since we had had our leaving do, and what seemed like an eternity since we had made the actual choice to leave for Australia. Of course, these things do take time; but after the dust had settled from the funeral, the question of leaving seemed more pressing than ever. Alongside it, my sense of frustration intensified.

What are we still doing here? What's holding us back?

We hit the road in the camper again, this time travelling around the east coast of Scotland. If I had felt a bit lost before, now that feeling really hit home. I had lost my mum, and even though we had all been poised for it to happen, I just felt very down and uncertain about the future. We still didn't know what was happening. I just felt powerless.

I now had no close blood relatives left in Scotland. My eldest son and my daughter lived on the other side of the world, and my youngest was travelling. Even the rugged beauty of the coast couldn't cut through the fug I was in. In fact, I don't have many strong memories from that second leg of travelling, which says a lot in itself. The question of the future dominated, and demanded an answer.

Why the hell would I want to live in Inverness anymore? What was the *point*?

Something had to give. We had been serious about leaving when we'd sold the house, but now I couldn't help but wonder if the whole thing was a big mistake. Nothing was definite. Maybe we should just buy a smaller house somewhere, cancel the whole damned thing.

Then again, we had sold the house. All our stuff was in storage. We had gotten all our jabs. Our kids were ready to host us down under. We had been planning it and talking about it for what seemed like an eternity. It was only the visa situation that was stopping us – one final, apparently unmoving hurdle.

With these kinds of thoughts gnawing at me, my resolve gradually sharpened. I was still feeling lost, but gradually became quite dogged in pursuit of a solution, checking all corners of the internet for a way we could get our visas. But as sometimes happens, the answer wasn't found through meticulous research – instead it dropped into my lap. One day I was chatting to Josie, the grandmother of Conor. Conor is a Scot too, originally from Denny before moving out to Australia.

"Have you seen this new visa you can get?" Josie said. "You can go to Australia on a year's holiday."

Wow! We'd missed this option. We looked it up online, and it was a new avenue. Andy wouldn't need to get clearance to work; it could all get sorted out while he was there. It would be a bit of a punt, admittedly, but worst-case scenario, we could just try it for a year. At least we would be *there*, actually in Australia, at long last.

"Let's just see what happens."

Our mentality shifted a little. It didn't need to be perfect. So we applied online. Then it was just a waiting game.

We were sat in the camper one day in September, when Andy looked up from his phone. There was a twinkle in his eye.

"What?"

"Well. I'm going to Australia."

"What?"

It had taken less than 48 hours for the confirmation to come through! We couldn't believe it. It was the green light, at last! But even more than that, where the hell was my confirmation?

"Where's my email? I want my email!"

I didn't have to wait too long. It came through soon enough, and all of a sudden we were sharing a moment – a moment in which we realised, *We're going!*

The money from our house was now tied up with a financial adviser, and we had a month to sell the camper and get Barney's jabs and paperwork sorted. We set the departure date for October, and bought our flights. Our wandering around the British Isles was over. Let the Australian odyssey begin!

4

PERTH, AUSTRALIA – NOT PERTH, SCOTLAND

(October 2017 to May 2018)

It was time to say goodbye. Goodbye to friends and family. Goodbye to the cats, who we sadly had to give to Cats Protection after 11 years with us. Goodbye to our old lives, and maybe goodbye to Scotland, once and for all.

I always knew it would be hard, but I could never have predicted just how hard. Saying cheerio to Sally, Andy's mum, was completely heart wrenching – even more so for Andy himself, though he'd never admit it! She's a retired nurse, so has plenty of practice at holding her emotions in check. When she started crying – well, it brought home what a huge change we were about to embark on. We would see each other again in five months, when Sally would fly out for Hazel and Conor's wedding. But she had done so much for us over the years, and at that moment five months felt like a lifetime.

One of the last social things we did before leaving was a barbecue, round at our friends Bob and Liz's house. Bob is also Andy's brother-in-law, and we've always gotten on so well. It was a nice September day. The food was lovely. And none of that really mattered, because I was just in bits. My prediction about it all being too painful was proven entirely accurate. I cried my eyes out.

"Come on Joy," Liz tried to comfort me. "It'll be OK."

"No it won't. I'll never see you again."

For me, goodbyes are hard – and this was one of the hardest. These people had been part of our lives, and we had been part of theirs, for so long. We would be seeing them again soon enough, but to think that we were moving so far away from them all was nearly unbearable.

But we had made our decision. For now, it was goodbye to the old and hello to the new.

A month later we were sat in Glasgow airport, eating breakfast, getting ready to fly. Things had moved so fast. It almost felt like the whole thing was a dream, but here we were ready to board the plane.

As a final cheerio I wrote a Facebook post, letting everyone know we were finally on our way. To my delight, a huge number of people posted encouraging comments in response.

"Come back soon!"

"We'll miss you – good luck out there!"

"We'll come to see you soon."

It was lovely seeing all those good wishes, but bittersweet too. After all, how soon was soon? Flying to Australia isn't like hopping on a quick flight to Europe. It's a long haul, and it's not cheap. Who knew how long it would be before we saw these people again?

Then, as it so often goes in airports, our gate was called and it was time to go. There was no time left for these thoughts – the plane was ready to fly, and so were we.

By now, the trip over to Australia was familiar enough – we had been a bunch of times in the last few years – but this time, we carried with us the knowledge that we had nothing to come back to. All our stuff was in storage, ready to be shipped over once we'd sorted things out. The house was sold, and we had said our goodbyes. This was it.

At Dubai, Barney was put on a separate flight to Melbourne – part of the quarantine procedure. In the end, with his extra stop off, our dog would end up seeing more of Australia than we did!

Fast forward 24 hours and we arrived at Perth airport. Hazel had come to meet us solo, as Conor was working offshore at the time. We were jetlagged, tired and hungry, but we were there! We hopped in her car for the drive back to their place, catching up the whole way home. This, of course, is where we first heard the question that would become the bane of our lives over the next six months: "So, what are you two gonna do?"

The truth is, we had no clue. Just getting there had been an ordeal enough – we were breathing a big sigh of relief, and future planning just wasn't on the agenda! Our idea had always been to move over to Australia so we could be nearer to the kids and see more of them. But in practice, we had jumped on the holiday visa option without any clear plan.

Wasn't it great to be here though? God, I had missed all the sunshine. Hazel and Conor were living in the Perth suburbs, and pretty soon we had slept off the flight and were settling into their home. It was springtime; the weather was light and sunny, with blue skies. The bright parakeets were flitting between the trees, squawking and chattering. We felt welcome straight away.

"What's the plan then?"

Oh, for God's sake.

Now it was Lewis's turn to be asking.

"There's no plan," I explained patiently. "If we just bum about for a year and then go back to Scotland, so be it."

He raised his eyebrows and nodded.

We were back in Dunsborough again, with all its gorgeous sandy beaches. A beach for every activity: one for surfing, one for sailing, another for walking. It may not have the shops like Perth, but my word it felt like paradise. Lewis was also away a lot, working offshore. But when he came back home we all got some real quality time together. It was great to see him.

Still, we remained in a strange position now we were here. We were bouncing around between our kids, unsure whether we were just on a long holiday or laying the foundations for something more permanent. As the excitement of the first few weeks turned into months, and spring segued into summer, Andy started looking for jobs. People carried on asking us what we were doing, of course, and the question continued to bring a certain pressure with it. We were, tentatively, asking ourselves the same questions.

Now we're here, can we figure out a way to stay here? Can we make a real go of this?

Before we knew it, Christmas was upon us – but as Lewis was working away, he couldn't spend it with us. We did manage Hogmanay though. Some of Lewis's friends flew out for it from Scotland, and we celebrated in Dunsborough. Then summer came to a close and, quite suddenly, it was nearly time for Hazel and Conor's wedding.

Hazel had arranged a bunch of dress fittings just after New Year, so we spent some lovely days out together getting that sorted, just mum and daughter. She was an absolute demon when it came to organising that wedding – every detail was covered. Honestly, Andy and I didn't need to lift a finger until the big day.

Truly, she did a fantastic job, and the wedding itself was absolutely wonderful. It took place outside at a beachside lodge down in Dunsborough, and they had booked five amazing suites for close friends and family, with hot tubs on the balconies. There was even a glamping area – the set up was just amazing. Four of Hazel's friends, whom she had known since her school days, flew out from Scotland to see her tie the knot. Hazel couldn't believe it; Australia is a big ask for someone to attend a wedding after all. But to her delight they were all there. Another old school friend, who had also moved out to Australia, played bagpipes as she walked down the aisle. Innis played guitar as everyone took their seats. There were so many beautiful details, which came together to make an unforgettable day.

I felt a tremendous sense of pride as I watched Andy walking Hazel down the aisle, the bagpipes swelling behind them. We may have been right on the western tip of the Aussie coast, but there was more than a hint of Scotland in the air that day. Not least the sheer number of kilts – there were loads! The boys had theirs on to see their sister get married, and the Aussies love a kilt anyway. Plenty of tartan doing the rounds.

When it came to the speeches, I was bricking it. We had, unintentionally, been staying with Hazel and Conor for about six months now, with a few trips to Lewis in between. Conor must be a saint. He hadn't complained once in the whole time we were there. But we felt so embarrassed about the situation, the fact we still hadn't gotten our feet on the ground. After saying a few lovely things about his new bride, Conor turned his gaze to us: "And now, the in-laws!"

God, this poor lad has put up with us for months on end... What's he gonna say?

Well, we needn't have worried: he had nothing but nice words to say. And fair enough, as he was part of the family now. We treat Conor like a son whenever we see him. Right then and there, though, I was just relieved that he didn't take the piss!

When it came to Andy's speech, I could clearly detect the same apprehension in Hazel. She must have been thinking, *Oh God...what's he gonna say?*

To his daughter's relief, Andy was also entirely charming. He told her how proud of her he was, pointing out all the amazing things she had already done in her life. Lovely sentiments all round. By the time the DJ came on and the Scottish dancing started I felt like I was floating on a cloud.

Then, just like that, it was over. The wedding had become something of a milestone for us during the first six months of our time down under. Even though we still didn't have any solid plans in place, it felt like Hazel and Conor's big day was a good enough reason for us to be there – which of course it was. But it had, perhaps, also been a bit of an excuse to avoid the painful question of the future. Now it was over... Well, we really did have to figure out what the hell we were doing.

Sally went back to Scotland, Lewis went back to work and Innis went off to New Zealand. Hazel and Conor weren't going on honeymoon until the end of April, so we headed to Lewis's for a while to give them a post-wedding breather. Andy and I were feeling even more guilty about the whole situation, especially now they were married. The newlyweds assured us it was fine by them, but still, we really didn't want to take the piss. We looked after the house for Lewis while he was away, and in the meantime Andy was firing off CVs every day – without any luck. Being on the wrong side of 55 he was getting quite a lot of knockbacks, but he kept up the momentum despite this.

Autumn came, and with it the cold and rain. As April drew to a close, we headed back up to Perth again to cat-sit for the newlyweds while they went on their honeymoon. Seven months of pinballing between Dunsborough and Perth... we were starting to feel like it would never end. Until, one day, Andy had some good news. In his campaign to find work, he had been firing off his CV further and further afield. By this point, we would take just about anything that seemed decent – never mind if it was in Perth, or even Western Australia. To say we were getting desperate is a bit of an overstatement, but what have you got? We'll take it!

This is how a man named Peter, CEO of Harvey Developments in Alice Springs, made contact. He explained that he had been impressed by Andy's CV, and would be interested in giving him a job at the company. Alice Springs was a long way away, but it was the first real bite we'd had.

"What do you reckon?" Andy asked me. "Shall we just go for it?"

As I've mentioned, I often agonise over tricky decisions like this. However, this time was different. We were already over halfway through our holiday visa.

"Well, what else do we do? We either go for it, or we throw in the towel and go home."

That was how it started – our ambition to live in the very heart of Australia. Alice Springs, a town of around 26,000 people, is bang in the middle of the continent, in what is known as the red centre. We decided to drive there from Perth to save money – it was only a few thousand kilometres, give or take! And then we were going to live and work there. All of a sudden, where there had been none at all, we had a plan.

We waited until the kids were back from their honeymoon before telling them. You might be able to imagine the tone of the conversation.

"We're going to Alice Springs."

"Oh, nice. You want to visit?"

"Nah. We're going to live there."

"You're going to live there?"

We explained the situation. We had one job offer on the table. There had been a few phone calls with Peter now, and he seemed keen to get us over to Alice as soon as feasible. Andy would be heading up the painting department of Harvey Developments. They would even provide us with accommodation. It was a solid offering.

But Hazel and Conor were dumbfounded.

"Mum," said Hazel, "of all the places in Australia, you wanna go to the red centre? It's literally the middle of nowhere!"

Conor, fair play to him, was very straight up about the disadvantages of our plan.

"I know guys who have worked out there," he told us. "It's a pretty intense place. They end up actually red – that red dust gets into their skin."

"We need to take this opportunity, guys," I explained. "Our minds are made up. But don't you worry – I'm not leaving until I see Harry and Meghan get married on the telly!"

So we had a couple more weeks with them before it was time to go. At first, God bless them, they really tried to dissuade us. As Conor appealed to Andy, "You don't have to do this. You don't know what Australians are like. They're completely different to British people, and especially Scottish people. They'll promise you the earth, but..."

"Conor, we cannot live here with you and Hazel forever more! You've only been married a month and the in-laws are already with you. It's not fair, on you or on us."

And it wasn't – I stand by that point. The two of them had been the most patient couple in the history of the world! You can't have your in-laws living with you like that for the indefinite future, you just can't. We were also living there rent-free. We would buy the kids' shopping, take them out for dinner. We would try to spend money on them, and they were like, "We don't want your money! You don't take money from us when we come to stay with you."

"But we're *living* with you!"

"Stay here. Don't go to Alice."

"We *can't* stay here!"

Round it went.

Harry and Meghan got married on a Saturday, 19th May. So in a way I got two weddings out of my first six months in Australia – not bad really. Then it was Sunday night, and we were prepped to leave the following morning. Finally, we were spreading our wings and branching out to start our new life.

Hazel and Conor gave us some gifts for the journey. Or perhaps 'supplies' would be more accurate: head torches, spare batteries, a first aid kit. Hazel had repurposed the box her wedding flowers had come in; she had written 'From Perth to Alice Springs' on the lid. Then she gave me a journal so I could keep a record of the trip. The inscription inside said: 'To Mum, Dad and Barney. This book is to record all your moans and groans and all your happy memories. Enjoy your big adventure – we can't wait to hear all about it. Lots of love, Conor, Hazel and the cats.'

That journal would indeed, by the end of the journey, be a chronicle of all the ups and downs we experienced. In fact, it became the basis of this very book.

Hazel and Conor's Wedding Day, 10th March

5

THE ROAD TO NOWHERE

(21st to 27th May 2018)

"Please stop at every garage you pass. Make sure you fill up on petrol all the time. And always get more water."

"Yes, OK."

Hazel gestured purposefully.

"Get a swag too."

Translation: a simple but practical two-person tent, designed to be built close to the ground.

"What are you gonna do if you park up? At least you'll have a swag you can sleep in then."

When your kids start trying to parent you...

"Swag?" I objected. "I'm not staying in a swag! I want to stay in hotels."

"There are no hotels, Mum! You're going through the feckin' desert!"

She wasn't wrong. The road between Perth and Alice cut right through over 1,000 kilometres of scrubby, red-gold wilderness: the infamous Nullarbor Plain and its surrounding territory. An unbroken expanse of, well, nothing.

Or nearly nothing. There are, of course, the infamous roadhouses that punctuate the highway through the desert. But to call them hotels would be the overstatement of the year, if not the century. Of course, while I may have high standards compared to some people, I soon got used to the reality of the sleeping arrangements. But how people actually manage to live at these places for the long term, I honestly do not know. They were very, very basic. The bare ingredients of shelter and comfort. One of the first ones we stayed in reminded me of a big shed. It didn't even have windows. Just four walls, a bed, a table and a light.

Still, it was better than spending a night in the swag by the side of the road. It was winter-time now, which meant nights were getting colder. One of the few features of the roadhouses you felt grateful for was the big chunky heaters over the beds – you certainly needed them at this time of year.

Our little car was our donkey, packed sky high. It was freighted with all our stuff – two small travelling cases that gave us easy access to necessities on the road, and two larger holdalls full of stuff we would unpack on arrival. Every time we stopped for the night, we had the elaborate ritual of unloading the car – because frankly, you have to be careful out on the road. It's a different kind of culture, and you can't trust anyone. There are a lot of thefts out there in the nothing. We were told as much by the servo owners – all you ever heard about was people filling up on petrol then doing a runner. There was a Wild West vibe to the whole thing.

From our point of view, everything we had in Australia was crammed into our luggage – the foundation of our new life in Alice Spring was in our car. We really couldn't afford to get robbed en route.

Our schedule was certainly gruelling. We were driving about 10 hours a day, finally stopping at a roadhouse just before dark. You couldn't risk driving the Nullarbor at night. Too much danger of a stray kangaroo or emu colliding with you and totalling your car –

and then you really would be screwed, stuck in the middle of bloody nowhere without a ride or a phone signal. Distance can make the difference between life and death out there. You can't mess about.

Still, even though the journey was a serious undertaking, as seasoned travellers Andy and I relished it. The whole challenge was one we were ready to embrace – partly because we love an adventure, and also because, on the other side of that treeless plain, our new life was waiting.

The first European to cross the Nullarbor was an English explorer named Edward John Eyre in 1841. It took us two Scottish explorers a bit longer to have a go, granted, but we certainly did it quicker than him, and via his namesake, the Eyre Highway (part of Highway 1). It took Eyre and his men about four months, in an ordeal which included dehydration, mutiny and murder. Andy and I got on each other's nerves from time to time, but stopped short of the rest. The point, however, is that the Nullarbor has quite a fearsome reputation. Writing about Eyre's expedition some 24 years later, Henry Kingsley described the plane as 'a hideous anomaly, a blot on the face of Nature, the sort of place one gets into in bad dreams'. Which seems a tad dramatic, if you ask me, but certainly there is something intimidating about it. Each day we would depart at about 9.30am: get packed up, drive out onto the road and see that, once again, it was a straight line that never seemed to end, disappearing into the horizon. There's something quite surreal about it, a road that just seems to go on forever, day after day; the feeling that the steering wheel is actually now redundant, because it's practically a straight line from here to eternity.

We travelled all day, only stopping for coffee, petrol and water at servos. Remarkably, water was more expensive than petrol – about three times more, in fact. That may seem ridiculous, until you remember you're travelling through an arid wasteland.

Despite how endless and barren it seemed, the truth was that the Nullarbor was also a haven for some. Wildlife, most obviously: a large portion of the plain has Wilderness Protection Status, and sustains 390 species of plant and many rare species of animal, including wombats, kangaroos, owls and bats. In practice, as our little silver Hyundai pootled along the never-ending highway, the most common sighting was roadkill. Plenty of dead roos came into sight along the way – far fewer live ones.

There are also people, incredibly, who have found their place in the world on the Nullarbor. When I spoke to one guy sitting at a fire outside a roadhouse, and asked how long he had lived out here, he replied, "Years."

"Do you like it?"

"Oh yeah!" He was an enthusiastic local. As he told it, he had been travelling over the plain, just like we were; he had stopped at this very roadhouse for a couple of nights, got offered a job, took it and never looked back.

I struggled to understand it.

"But there's no shops! You're in the middle of the desert, there's nothing at all."

"Oh yeah, but we just put an order in to Coles to get supplies," he said matter-of-factly. "The lorry comes every Friday."

So that was how it worked, in practice. A scattering of other houses near to the roadhouse, which constituted a community of sorts. A community that relied – 100% – on drop offs from Coles. He didn't seem to get the main thrust of my point – that there was nothing bloody there. Or maybe I was missing the point, because that was what he wanted, in the end.

On it went. A sparse string of makeshift settlements with quirky names: Cocklebiddy, Eucla, Yalata. The endless horizon, the vast wasteland all around. But there was also the coast, not too far away. The Nullarbor stretches along the Great Australian Bight, a region of coast that really does look like a shallow bite taken out of the bottom of the country. And, as if the experience of crossing such a landscape wasn't surreal and disorientating enough, it's here you can find the world's longest golf course. The Nullarbor Links ranges some 1,365 kilometres along the southern coast, with 18 holes dotted between each of the route's roadhouses and settlements. You can basically come off the Eyre Highway at designated points and play a hole of golf. Not having brought our clubs, and not being particularly keen golfers anyway, we chose to give it a miss. I just found myself wondering who cut the greens.

We also took plenty of photos of the sea as we passed around the Bight, as there's just something a bit weird about this intense, arid heat and dusty scrubland being contrasted with all that wild ocean.

The Nullarbor is a true slice of wilderness, one in which human comforts are hard won. Dog comforts too, for that matter. Barney, our furry, faithful friend, was the easiest travelling companion we could have asked for. Most of the time he just dozed in the back of the car for hours on end. But again, you had to be careful out here. Halfway through the journey we stopped at the Nullarbor Roadhouse for the night. Stepping out of our room to go in search of a bite to eat, we came face to face with a dingo – our first really up-close encounter. I was struck by what beautiful dogs they are, with friendly faces and lovely red coats. They don't look menacing in the slightest. Quite the opposite; they look friendly. Being by itself, this dingo darted off as soon as it saw us. But we would soon learn they're a far less timid animal in a pack. In fact, they're well known for enticing domestic dogs into playing with them. Which sounds lovely, until you learn that it's actually a ploy to get your dog away, so they can kill it. It's pretty devious, and pretty horrible. The poor domestic dog must be thinking, Oh great, I've got some friends to play with! Then suddenly, the pack attacks. Suffice to say, we kept a very close eye on Barney during the trip.

You've got to be wary of kangaroos too. Everyone thinks, Oh, kangaroos are really cute! But if one jumps into the road you can get in a very nasty accident. Even if there isn't a collision, you've got to be careful, because they're big. If you get too near they'll get up on their back legs and box you! You see it in the cartoons and it's true – they stand six feet tall and suddenly they're not so cute anymore.

On another note, when was the last time you used a proper paper map to navigate somewhere, rather than your phone? Going through the middle of nowhere means you're genuinely cut off from the rest of the world: no phone signal, no internet. Just you, your car and the road ahead, for hours on end. We had our map of central Australia to hand, in case we got lost... but then, how could we? It was a straight line, the whole way. The map showed when a servo or roadhouse was coming up though, which was handy.

Space matters on the Nullarbor, and so does time. As we moved through the different regions, we gradually moved through the corresponding time zones. At Cocklebiddy a sign informed us we were 45 minutes ahead of Perth – please put your watch forward! Then, from Australia Western Standard Time we moved on another 45 minutes, to Australia Central Standard Time. That meant we were officially in South Australia – and on Alice Springs time! We weren't sure what to expect at the border. Barney got waved through, no problem at all. But some details can't be overlooked.

"Have you got any fruit or veg or any sort of edibles?"

"Um, well we've got an Esky."

Everyone in Australia has an Esky – a small portable fridge that preserves your food and drink against the sweltering heat. They wanted to have a look, and upon opening it they soon found the culprits: our apples and bananas! Confiscated immediately. Honestly, I thought it was bonkers. Do they really think the fruit flies in my fridge are going to infect the whole of South Australia?

Anyway, even without our fruit we were now well on our way. It was a Wednesday; we were halfway there, with just three more days of driving left. The terrain started to change; we could see trees again, for a start. The landscape was a little greener, less foreboding. The Nullarbor was behind us.

That night we stopped at Kimba – which put us halfway across Australia, as a sign in town proudly declared. We stayed at the Kimba Roadhouse, run by an Indian family, and had a good curry for our tea that night. We needed it; by our estimate we still had another 14 hours of driving before we reached Alice Springs.

First, though, we turned our faithful little car north, to Coober Pedy (perhaps the prize winner among those weird Aussie names I love!). This town is known as the world's opal capital: it provides about 70% of the global supply of the precious stone. Most of the town is underground. So much of it has been used for mining over the years – and the heat is so oppressive – that it seems only natural that large sections of the ground have been hollowed out to house shops, homes and facilities. A whole community underground. We were excited to take a look around this weird and wonderful place, but of course we had nowhere to leave Barney. When we finally found a hotel that allowed pets, we faced another issue. Our wee car had just struggled up a rough and rocky road. The manager came to meet us.

"Oh, we've just booked a room – we've got our dog with us as well."

"Oh yeah – you can chain your dog up over there."

He pointed to a wall.

"We're not chaining our dog up anywhere, pal. You said you were pet friendly. Our dog comes with us!"

"No he bloody doesn't!"

"Well, we're not staying if we can't take the dog in the room."

"But you've booked!"

"Yeah. But I'm telling you now we're not staying. You're not getting a deposit; you're getting nothing! I'm even going to go online and bad mouth ya!"

He was so angry, but that sealed it. We turned the car around and left. To be honest, we hated Coober Pedy. It was just stony and grey and a bit grubby – we were quite glad to leave. We were typical Scottish with that bloke, really. But our dog was not getting chained up anywhere, at any time. One thing I learned during my time in Australia was that Aussies and Scots do tend to clash. Or at least, with these Scots they do. I do think that a lot of the white men in Australia are just plain ignorant. They don't know anything else but Australia, and they don't want to.

"Oh, we're going on holiday."

"Where are you going?"

"Oh, we're going to Adelaide... or Melbourne, or Sydney."

"Don't you ever leave Australia?"

"Oh, what's the point of leaving Australia? Our country's the best!"

"Wouldn't you ever like to see Europe?"

"Oh, it's too far to go!"

The following morning we hit the road at 9am, and faced down the final stretch to Alice Springs. Just eight hours later, after a couple of servo stops, we arrived. I had been writing notes in the diary Hazel got me throughout the journey, just little snapshots of our experience. On that day I wrote: 'Arrived at 5pm, the next chapter begins.' That was all; but it summed up the whole feeling as we drove into Alice and completed our cross-country odyssey. We had survived the outback, and had a few tales to tell along with it. We were feeling pretty pleased with ourselves – and fair enough. It had been one of the most epic journeys of our lives.

The start of the journey…

Barney all set for his travels

The Nullarbor — no trees

The road to nowhere

WELCOME TO MADURA

WEST	KMS
COCKLEBIDDY	91
CAIGUNA	157
BALLADONIA	338
NORSEMAN	529
ESPERANCE	736
KALGOORLIE	731
PERTH	1249

EAST	
MUNDRABILLA	116
EUCLA	180
BORDER	196
NULLABOR	382
NUNDROO	524
PENONG	603
CEDUNA	676
PORT AUGUSTA	1444
ADELAIDE	1456

Cocklebiddy, roadhouse

Getting to South Australia

The Nullarbor — the longest golf course

Heading to Pt Augusta not Fort Augustus

NULLARBOR LINKS GOLF COURSE
DINGO'S DEN

Welcome to

NULLARBOR ROADHOUSE
SOUTH AUSTRALIA

The quarantine checkpoint where we lost our apples and bananas

First time we saw 'Alice Springs'

6

A HARD WELCOME

(27th to 28th May 2018)

Six months after we got back to Scotland, as the COVID-19 pandemic reached the UK and everything went into lockdown, I couldn't help but be reminded of Alice Springs. After all, Andy and I had existed in a sort of permanent lockdown there – surrounded by high fences, feeling quite cut off from the unfamiliar world outside. Social distancing had been par for the course, because we had hardly known anyone in the town.

We had started with high hopes. After the six-day road trip across the Nullarbor, we were tired but buoyed by the excitement of what would be waiting for us. Alice Springs really had felt like the promised land – and hadn't we been promised a decent set-up? Andy would soon be helming the Harvey Developments painting division, and there was a flat waiting for us, supplied by the company. Peter's frequent phone calls when we were in Perth had been positive, encouraging. God willing, we would soon be on our way to a working visa, swiftly followed by a permanent residency visa (known as a PR) – the Holy Grail of documents. If we could secure those, we would be free to move about and work wherever we wanted to, without sponsorship.

The letters PR spelled 'freedom'.

So yes, we were feeling pretty optimistic. Maybe that was our first mistake.

When we got to Alice Springs, we were met by Peter and a man named Graham, the company's white South African manager.

"Oh yes, we've got the flat for you above the office."

Graham took us up to show us. Honestly, after nearly a week on the road we were knackered. We couldn't wait to just crash out for the rest of the day and start our Alice Springs experience properly tomorrow.

"Well, this is it," he said awkwardly. "It's not the best flat in the world, I won't lie to you."

Eh?

"But we'll see you on Monday," he continued. "You'll have the weekend to get settled in."

As welcoming speeches went, it wasn't exactly a classic. Then off he went, leaving us standing at the door, ready to look inside.

I could have leapt. From first sight, the flat was awful. Really grubby – it clearly hadn't been cleaned in a long time. As we walked around and got the measure of the place, my heart just sank. It was nothing less than a total shithole.

Some key features in the horror show: two dirty reclining armchairs – I had to spray and wipe them before we could sit in them; a pile of furniture – dining room table and chairs literally heaped on top of each other like a jumble sale, half the chairs broken, unusable; unmade beds, which looked as if someone might have been sleeping in them just a few minutes ago; stained mattresses lurking underneath the covers.

The flat had three bedrooms, and they were all disgusting. The curtains hung limp and askew off two of the bedroom windows. Everything seemed ancient, knackered, dirty... unfit for wildlife, let alone humans. It was an utter nightmare, and the more we explored the more we found. The kitchen, painted bright orange like something out of the 1960s, complete with Formica, made me want to vomit. Neither of us could believe it. After nearly a week of travel, we had arrived at a proper hovel – our new home was worse than some of the roadhouses we'd stayed in.

Evidently our first priority would be to clean the hell out of it tomorrow. But what about tonight? The thought of spending our first night in those grubby bedsheets…

That's when we had the bright idea to use the swag. Hazel's suggestion that we might need it on the road had never transpired, thankfully – there had been no nights on the hard shoulder under the stars, worrying about dingoes – but we were extremely grateful for it now! The Australian outback? No problem, not needed. The 'comforts' of our new place? No question, unpack that thing!

Swags are not known for being especially spacious, but once we had put it up in one of the bedrooms and given it a quick brush, we were ready to sleep. Not exactly the comfortable welcome we had been hoping for, but still so much better than those beds, trust me. Barney joined us, flopping at our feet after we had settled down.

The next morning, we took a wary look at the place again; maybe we had been tired the night before, overreacting? Nope. I turned to Andy.

"I can't live here. It's a complete and utter shithole!"

"Right. Let's head down to Coles and get some cleaning stuff."

Coles is of course the local supermarket, an Aussie chain you can find just about everywhere. From the squalor of the flat we ventured out into Alice for the first time. It was the tail end of autumn, right on the cusp of winter – but my God, it was hot.

It was a reminder of just how far inland we were now, right at the dusty red centre. This wasn't Perth anymore. Thankfully, Coles was under a cover to cool you down a bit, but even on a Sunday the place was buzzing. Every inch of the supermarket was rammed with shoppers. It was our first real encounter with the town, and it was all quite disorientating.

Is this what it's going to be like all the time?

What's more, I have to be honest about something. Alice Springs is a very Aboriginal town – and stepping into Coles was, I think, our first real experience of culture shock. Remember, we're from the north of Scotland, a fairly small area without many people. Not a hugely diverse place, either. Alice was the total opposite of what we were used to, and frankly it knocked me sideways. Aboriginals everywhere – the noise of them, yakking away, and the smell of them! It hit you like a wall. Not the cleanest of people, and somebody would later tell Andy they eat a lot of kangaroo meat and the smell comes out in their skin. You know, it's a hot place; you sweat a lot. There was a lot of body odour doing the rounds in that supermarket.

I won't lie, I was just quite taken aback. Cultural differences can have a big impact, and my first impression was that the people just seemed like a different breed. They had such different faces, and they were all wearing black in spite of the heat. I was fascinated, but also pretty intimidated. I had never been so conscious of being different – a different colour, a different race and culture. And yes, it was frightening. We were strangers in a strange land.

Coles was a whirlwind of activity, and at some point during the trip Andy and I got split up. As I wandered down one of the aisles, I came face to face with a big group of teenage boys – black, Aboriginal boys. There must have been about six or seven of them, all crowded together, taking up all the space.

For a moment, I froze.

What am I going to do? How am I gonna walk past them?

Again, I just didn't know what to expect. I suppose it was fear of the unknown. So I kept to the very edge of the aisle, heading past them carefully – and suddenly, to my surprise, they all stepped back from me instead.

Our eyes met.

"Oh, sorry! We didn't see you there!"

I stopped in my tracks, and it was only then that I realised how rude I had been to them. I had been prejudiced, and based on what, exactly? All these negative stories you hear about Aboriginals in the media, mostly.

Gosh – they're actually so mannerly.

I suddenly felt quite embarrassed by my own assumptions – that I had seen them as a threat. This little exchange was proving me completely wrong. I gave them a smile back as I passed. In that moment, I felt myself warming to Alice Springs for the first time.

Maybe this place isn't as bad as it seems.

Andy and I met up again at the till.

"You're very busy today – are you always like this?" I asked the cashier.

"Oh, there's this big football match on," he explained.

We hadn't known, of course, but it was a big deal for the locals, which explained the packed supermarket on a Sunday morning. Such sporting entertainment was not for the likes of us, though. Oh no: we had a flat to clean.

I was still processing what had happened with the young lads in the aisle on our way back to the car, when we had another encounter. As mentioned, we had heard quite a lot already about the reputation that Aboriginals have in Australia. Graham had told us the night before to watch where we went shopping, as the local IGA (Independent Grocers Australia) was known for Aboriginals hanging around and pestering people for money. That's why we had gone to Coles, on his advice. There are clearly still huge problems with race and racism in Australia, but being new in town we had taken the tip at face value – we didn't want to get caught up in anything we didn't understand. The Aboriginals have a lot of their own languages, which we didn't realise until Andy started working with them. Graham had told us that you sometimes think they're talking to you, when they're actually shouting across the street to their mates.

I think it's fair to say we were on our guard. Of course it's prejudiced, but when you're outsiders you pay close attention to whatever info you find. You don't take chances with this sort of stuff.

But on the way back to the car, we saw a young Aboriginal man holding an absolutely gorgeous baby. He had a big grin on his face as he played with her, bouncing her up and down. It was such a lovely sight. A young dad, playing with what we assumed was his kid. We exchanged a few words and a smile – and once again, all my prejudices were just torpedoed. We might be on the other side of the world, in a wildly different culture. But in actual fact, the people here were, at heart, no different from those back home. That exchange, with the young man holding his baby, could have taken place back in Inverness. It could have been just the same with the lads in the aisle – in fact, they probably wouldn't have been nearly as respectful back home!

We had a carload of cleaning products and a day of scrubbing ahead of us, but much as the filthy flat had set my teeth on edge, I couldn't help but feel elated after those two small exchanges at Coles. We had made it over the Nullarbor in one piece. We had successfully stocked up on our first supply run, and had our first interactions. And today we would blitz that flat, doing whatever we could to make it liveable.

We were here, in Alice Springs. We had arrived.

Our swag

One of the first sunsets in Alice Springs

7

LEARNING TO LOVE THE UNKNOWN

(May to October 2018)

It's such a funny thing, how somewhere can be so familiar yet totally alien at the same time.

When we had emerged from the desert and arrived in the town at the very heart of Australia, it had been a total relief – quickly replaced by total hostility: towards our horrible flat, the locals, all these new and unfamiliar things we weren't used to. But it didn't take long before all those little, uncanny details started to chew at us, and made us see things a different way.

They would play British songs on the radio. 'Shotgun' by George Ezra was a favourite – it was a jingle on one of the stations, and quickly became a tune I will forever associate with Alice Springs. But then, straight after a song you knew, they had their own chat show that people could phone in to, and it was all in Aboriginal. It was just an interesting blend, one that summed up the mixture of cultures. At first it was very strange indeed, but pretty soon I found that I was warming to it.

Perhaps the strangest thing of all was how much Alice reminded me of Nairn, the small Scottish seaside town where Andy's mum Sally lived. They're both quite small places, geographically, and I soon started to see quite a parallel between them. Just swap out the Scottish weather for glorious sunshine and the pigeons for parakeets and you'd barely know the difference.

There was a point at which the comparison stopped, however.

For all its quietness, Nairn feels like a real community. It's easy to get to know your neighbours there, and for them to become friends. I really like to know my neighbours, and I like to gossip. I won't apologise for it.

In Alice, that just seemed impossible. First, there were loads of high fences. Everybody had those up – you couldn't see into people's gardens – and everyone had dogs. The post boxes aren't on your door, they're out front near the street, so you didn't even get to see your postie. Before we arrived, just about everyone had said to us, "Oh, it'll have a great community feel!" We were hoping for the same, of course. A fairly small town right in the middle of Australia – it wasn't like we were moving to Sydney. But no, community remained elusive throughout our time there.

In truth we were the outsiders, and maybe we just didn't mix. I didn't want to join clubs to get to know people. I wanted it to happen more naturally. But for the first six months in that flat, we really struggled to make any good connections. Plus, we were Scottish! The locals couldn't make us out. They'd look us up and down, trying to think of a question to ask that would say, "You're different, ain't cha?" They were totally confused by us.

I remember one day I went to the local supermarket. I was chatting to a guy about the fruit and veg, which hadn't come in that day. There had been some issue with delivery. As I was leaving he suddenly went, "Oi."

I went, "OK..."

"Where are you from?"

"Oh, I'm from Scotland. From the Highlands, way up where the Loch Ness monster lives."

"I'm just back from there."

I couldn't believe it. I mean, what are the chances? He had been over to Invergordon on holiday, a stone's throw from Nairn and Inverness. It was just surreal; while we had been gunning across the Nullarbor, the guy at the local supermarket had been in our neck of the woods.

The same thing happened with our estate agent, Sam, who had been over to Inverness a little while before we met him. It was just a little reminder that, no matter how small the place you come from is, you can always find a connection.

From the start, there was something fishy about Andy's job. At first he couldn't legally work, because Harvey Developments had yet to sort out his visa. So, rather than hitting the ground running as we had hoped, he spent the first couple of months in the office helping out. It was hardly the grand position Peter had described, though at least we got some time to explore Alice together.

Thankfully, when the ball finally got rolling the visas came through in a flash. In fact, our lady at the immigration office said it was the fastest approval she'd ever seen.

After the slow start, Andy went straight into it – and straight out of Alice, into the middle of bloody nowhere. We had known that Harvey Developments did a lot of work out in the countryside, the rural parts of the Northern Territory and South Australia. But we hadn't been told what the job would actually entail: Five or six hour drives out into the bush, to work on the most far-flung properties for days on end.

Andy had signed up for the role of Painting Manager – and had been told he would be running the painting department. In practice, he was the painting department – apart from contractors, Harvey Developments had just one other permanent worker whom Andy could manage. It was just him, the van, the tools and a rotating cast of lads – a far cry from the deal he'd been promised.

"Go on the tools, just so we can see what your work's like. Work on the tools to start with." That had been the rough outline of the invitation from Peter. "You'll be the manager of the painting department of the company – I need that for all the painters that work for me."

A pack of lies. Instead, Andy soon twigged that he would be bouncing from A to B, long drives followed by longer shifts. Sometimes he would arrive to find he needed to clean the house before it could be painted.

"So, what's the painting department like?" I asked after his first proper day.

"Well, it's just me and this other guy, to be honest..."

It was just iffy. Andy had run his own business for 28 years – and he got most of his work by word of mouth. He never even had to advertise, his reputation was so good. Sometimes people would stop him in the street, based on the quality of his work, and ask him to do their house too. On one occasion when this happened, and he offered to give the lady an estimate, she said, "I don't want an estimate – you must be really good if you're working for that couple, because we know just how fussy they are!"

He's just so good at his job.

Now though, he'd been reduced to a long-haul cleaning service. He was driving and on the tools every day, covering all the labour, not managing a department. It was a piss take.

To make matters worse, there was animosity from the get-go. Peter had been reassuring to us, and seemed like a nice enough guy at first. Graham, the South African, was another story. He soon proved himself to be quite a nasty little man. Frankly, he seemed to view Andy as a threat.

It wasn't even like you had to look for warning signs with this guy, it was so bleeding obvious how vindictive he was. One day, early on in the job, Andy was in the company offices when Graham came over. They'd barely met, but Graham launched straight into a really ugly, foul-mouthed tirade. He called Andy an effing B, effing C – every name under the sun. Andy's a very reasonable guy; this was not a reasonable conversation. Andy is also a black belt in karate – not someone you want to pick a fight with. Not that he's violent, but the threat is there, and when someone talks to you like that...

He avoided a direct confrontation that day, instead bringing the issue to Peter and explaining what Graham had said. Peter was horrified, outraged.

However, the next day Andy decided to go one further. He approached Graham in the car park and made it clear where he stood.

"If you've got a problem with me, let's sort this out now. Right here."

Graham looked bewildered, shrunk.

"Ah no, no – I don't mean it like that!"

Could it have been a misunderstanding? An attempt at banter turned sour? It's possible, but we don't think so. From all the evidence, it really seemed like he didn't want Andy in the company. He was nasty to him from day one. On another occasion he turned around and said, "You will never be a manager as long as I work here."

This to the man who was meant to be Painting Manager of the firm. It was disrespectful and a disgrace, and set the stage for what would follow.

Still, it was a job. Neither of us were happy with the set-up – far from it. But the pay was good, and our hopes of staying in Australia, of being nearer the kids, was riding on Andy's position. Harvey Developments would sponsor us, so the story went; but of course, there would need to be a good relationship and a satisfied employer for that to evolve into our PRs. Until then, the company had huge power over our future in Australia. We were stuck between a rock and a hard place, and we would just need to do the best we could under the circumstances.

Even more than that, we needed to learn to love the unknown. Not the easiest thing when you're pushing 60 and know just how you like things to be. But here wasn't home, and we would have to compromise. We'd need to adapt to Alice, and Andy's work, and Australia in order to build a happy life here. Clearly, it wasn't going to be easy.

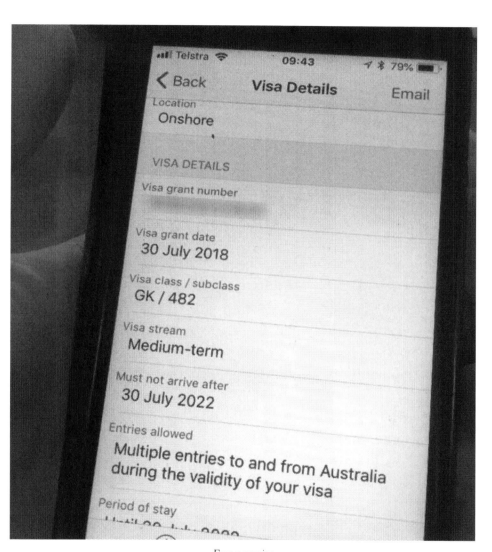

Four-year visa

8

THE GREAT AUSTRALIAN HOUSE HUNT

(September to November 2018)

For six long months, we slept in the swag. The kids would say to us, "Why don't you just go and buy a new mattress?" But we didn't need one – all our stuff was still with Pickfords, the movers in the UK. Until we had our permanent resident visas sorted, we couldn't risk bringing it all over. Instead, we were paying a small fortune each month just so Pickfords could keep hold of it.

And the visa situation? Worryingly quiet. If you didn't think too much about it, everything was fine: Andy was sponsored and had a job, we had money coming in, we had made the dream move. Stop just for a moment to check the facts, though, and it was clear we were in an unsatisfying situation. Andy was away for days on end, driving and working long hours in the back of beyond. Meanwhile I was by myself a lot of the time, and I didn't know anybody. I was isolated, starting to go slightly crazy, and when Andy came back he came back to this place. In a nutshell, things were bloody horrible. Our future – our hope for a decent life here – was completely in the hands of the company.

Which didn't seem to give a shit. Despite all his reassurances, Peter hadn't given us anything concrete to show that a permanent residency visa was in the works. It was all just platitudes, and it was starting to ring hollow. We needed something to happen, and soon.

Andy had been speaking to Peter about the situation, and I to his wife Jenny.

"Oh, are you OK in that flat upstairs?" she asked.

"The shithole?"

I can be very diplomatic when I need to be.

She laughed, but I pushed the point. "That's really what it is, Jenny. We don't even have beds we can sleep in."

The thing is, the flat was rent-free. Mind you, we certainly wouldn't have paid rent for it. But it felt like we didn't have much comeback, because we weren't paying for it. Having said that, we were paying for electricity and hot water – which included the company offices below us. There was an electricity box outside, and we had to buy these cards and feed them into the meter. They would leave the air conditioning on in the office all night, which annoyed us. Our money was paying for it.

The whole arrangement felt very unfair to us, and when we did bring it up, Peter and co always had an excuse to hand. Never mind the simple fact that they had given us somewhere to live that was nigh on unliveable. With things already feeling tense between Andy and Graham, we didn't want to push too hard. It was a delicate matter.

So we simply endured. The big telly in the living room was our saviour through the winter, into spring. It was a portal we could escape through into another dimension.

At one point, we also had to vacate the flat for about nine days, as Peter wanted to give it to some visiting workers as accommodation. He called them grubs; well, that was certainly appropriate for our flat.

"Can you not put them up somewhere else?" Andy asked. "We're living in that flat, aren't we?"

"No, no – I want them in the flat," Peter insisted.

So, for over a week we relocated to a nearby campsite. It was nice to have a break from the flat, of course. But that wasn't the point. We really didn't have a home to live in. After the nine days Peter announced we could move back into the flat.

"Ah, fantastic – back to the shithole then!"

It quickly became apparent that we would have to find a place of our own. While there wasn't much more we could do about the visa, we certainly could do something about our living situation. Even with the uncertainty of the future, we had come to Australia to make a proper go of it – and that meant we had to start thinking about laying down some roots. Plus, we simply had to get out of the flat. No amount of cleaning products could remedy the place, and our complaints to Peter and co had been ignored. For six months we had slept in the swag like nomads, and ordered takeaway food after seeing mice in the kitchen. We were sick to death of it; it wasn't real living.

So began our Alice Springs house hunt. As you may have guessed, I am just a little bit picky about where I live. I need to really connect with the feeling of the place, so that I can imagine myself actually living there. If there isn't that chemistry with a property from the off, forget it. And I hate, with a passion, places that haven't been cleaned and tidied. You are never going to sell me somewhere dirty!

That didn't stop them trying though. We got in touch with an estate agent, and at first a woman named Caroline was looking after us. Some of the places we ended up looking at were just unbelievable. As in, I cannot believe people could actually live there. One of them, owned by a Chinese guy, had all these old mattresses laying on the floor, and stacks of carry-out boxes piled up high. The smell was awful.

"Oh, I think they must sleep in this room... that's all they do here." No kidding!

She took one look at me and said, "Joy, I can tell by your face you don't like it here." So they realised pretty quickly that I'm not the sort of customer you can fob off with a shithole – we had already had six months of that. I had no tolerance for a so-called fixer-upper – at least not a dirty one. Some of the fixer-uppers they showed us even shocked Andy, who does that sort of thing for a living. They would try to sell you anything. They'd say things like, "Oh, you know what I would do with a place like this?" And then make some useless suggestion, to try to win us over, when the place was a total dump! Knock the wall down, put a partition up... why the hell would we invest $400,000 on a house if we had to do all that before it was even liveable?

It was quite an ordeal – and again, some of the cultural differences caused issues. On one occasion another estate agent, called Dominic, showed us round a nice place in Gillen, one of Alice's suburbs, which had an outdoor pool. I loved it. Really just wanted it straight away. So later that night, after the viewing, we went back to the house, knocked on the door and tried to do a sneaky deal ourselves. Unfortunately, the owner wasn't up for it – she wanted us to go through the estate agent. OK, not a problem, never mind. But the next day, when we went to their office, Dominic started raging!

"You don't do that here! What were you thinking?"

We were like, "Look pal, we're Scottish. You can't tell us what to do, and in Scotland it's a totally different process anyway when you're buying a house."

It got quite heated.

The thing was, we were new in town and desperate to get out of that flat, to get our feet on the ground with our own set up. As soon as we had it sorted, we could bring our stuff over and actually live. We didn't want to mess around – we just wanted it done. But by the same token, we weren't going to get ripped off.

However, when you're not a permanent resident it's almost inevitable that you will be. We found out that we would have to pay a ridiculous fee to the Foreign Investment Review Board (FIRB) to even make an offer on the house we liked. So that took the wind out of our sails. The house with the pool was in demand and we lost our chance to buy it. Just as we had found a place we liked, we had ended up in another bureaucratic rut. It was hugely frustrating.

Still, we were on a roll with the house hunting now, and we weren't gonna stop. You've got to hustle to get a decent place – and, sure enough, after a few more viewings we found another candidate. But it wasn't dirty tenants or fractious estate agents we had to worry about this time.

For some reason, there are no small houses in Alice Springs, or at least none that we saw. They all look like the places you used to see in Aussie soaps like Home and Away and Neighbours. This one, on Spearwood Road, had four bedrooms and two bathrooms, and just felt like a good find from the get-go. It belonged to an old boy who lived there alone, and when we went for the viewing we ended up feeling quite sorry for him. He was just sitting there in his house by himself – he seemed a bit down. He told us he was a widower, and his son lived miles away; he'd sometimes drive from Alice all the way to Adelaide in a oner, 14 hours on the road. I couldn't help but feel bad for him – clearly his son didn't really care much about him, letting him drive all that way. Why was he selling his house on his own? We spent a fair bit of time chatting to him, and later on decided we would make an offer. To our delight, he quickly accepted.

As you might imagine, I was very excited. The house needed a fair bit of work, but it was lovely – just the sort of thing we were after. I couldn't resist telling the kids, "Google Spearwood Road! Do it!"

"Wow. Looks like you found a nice house then."

"Yep. And soon we'll be moving in!"

It was September 2018. Andy got in touch with Pickfords, to tell them they could finally start shipping our stuff over. All the pieces were falling into place.

Can you feel the sting in the tail coming? Well, perhaps we got a bit carried away. Perhaps it was all a bit too good to be true.

Buying a house in Australia is a different experience compared with back home, as I've mentioned – there are a few more hoops to jump through. After you make the initial offer and that's been accepted, you work with a conveyancer to get a survey of the house. Then you go back to the landlord with a reduced price, which reflects the work that needs doing. So it's a two-step process – the initial offer usually isn't the final price.

It was in the middle of all this that things got weird. Having chatted to the old boy for a bit, we decided to go back to the house for another visit. It was all perfectly pleasant – he seemed more than happy that we were buying from him. But at the end of the visit, a strange, small detail stuck out. Andy shook his hand. He was a frail old man, so Andy gripped his forearm when they shook, to support him. But, for all intents and purposes, it was just a polite goodbye handshake.

Well, not to the old landlord. In fact, the handshake meant something quite specific to him. For reasons we still can't quite fathom, he got it into his head that Andy was a Freemason. That forearm handshake was – apparently – a secret gesture!

Of course, we were oblivious to all this. The buying process for the house continued as per normal. We worked with the conveyancer, and explained that we wanted to reduce the offer price because there was loads wrong with the house. It was going to cost a lot of money to get it fixed up – about $30,000 dollars all in. It was a substantial mark down.

One day, while all this is going on, we get a call from the estate agent.

"We don't know why, but there's a sealed letter from the seller waiting here for you. Can you come in and take a look?"

A what?

They wanted us to open it there and then – they were just being nosy of course. But we said no, it was his letter to us and we would open it in private. We took it home to read – and couldn't believe what it said.

The old boy revealed that he was a Freemason, part of the Lewis house. He had been some sort of doctor before he retired. The problem, again, was that handshake. He had taken it to be a sign that Andy too was a mason, and that the handshake had been a secret communication, an agreement between them that finalised the price for the house! Now, with the conveyancers asking for $30,000 off, he accused Andy of having tricked him.

The letter was two pages long, and extremely detailed. We still have it back in Alice Springs. 'A mason's word is his bond', he wrote. By bartering on the price, that bond had been broken! We were completely flabbergasted.

"I mean... is he serious?"

"He's serious about the price, that's for sure."

The estate agent couldn't believe it either. They said they'd never seen anything like it, in fact. So very weird. To this day we still don't know if it was a genuine misunderstanding, or a strange attempt to wriggle out of the price reduction.

All we knew was, if he was as serious as his letter suggested, we were in a tricky predicament. Our stuff would soon be on its way over, and we didn't yet have a moving date. The old boy had accepted our offer, but now there was this sudden U-turn with the conveyancing and the masonic ritual. I felt myself starting to panic a bit.

"Andy, it's been over two weeks since this all started. We need to get it sorted before our stuff arrives."

"Yeah, right enough."

We called the conveyancer, a lovely lady named Helen. She was English, but had been living in Australia for some years; she had her mum and dad moving over, so she knew what we were going through and was so helpful about it all. She reached out to the old boy, but things really had soured. He wouldn't sign the papers; in fact he wouldn't even communicate with her. He was stonewalling the whole thing.

The estate agent had no luck either – he wouldn't even answer the door to them, or his phone, or his email.

"Well... what do we do? How do we handle a situation like this?"

"Basically, you don't have a house."

It was a blunt and bitter pill to swallow. We had reached an impasse. The old boy doggedly refused to accept that Andy wasn't a mason, that there was some kind of misunderstanding. He insisted we had done him wrong, and it was soon clear that the whole house sale had floundered.

We didn't have time to wait, or for delicate diplomacy. We needed a house, pronto. It was going to be a little over two months before Pickfords sent our stuff over. The clock was ticking. Barney also complicated matters, as there are even more hoops to jump through when you've got a dog in tow. We needed a detached house to meet regulations, which was much harder to find. Things were looking stark.

What if our stuff turns up and there's nowhere for it to bloody go?

It was at this point that we met Sam, a new estate agent. Caroline was retiring, and he was her replacement. By now, I was getting really tired of all this. We had had the rug pulled out from under us twice, and we still didn't have our own house. Now, another estate agent was promising us they'd fix it – but would they, really? We were stuck in house hunting purgatory. It just felt like it would never end.

Indeed, Sam didn't inspire a huge amount of confidence at first. The first place he showed us was another fixer-upper – one that needed so much work that even Andy balked at the idea of buying it. I was at the end of my tether.

"No worries," Sam said. "I've got an idea of what you like now. I'll keep you in mind."

I said, "No you won't. I can tell you estate agent after estate agent has said that. Nobody has ever kept us in mind."

"No, I will."

"We'll see."

I was sick with the lot of them – and I think, honestly, I was so pissed off about the whole thing that I phased out a bit.

The next house Sam took us to was what's known as a base house. There's a highly restricted American military base in Alice, and a whole load of houses were built for the staff. They're all built the same way – spacious interiors with the rooms all leading into one another. The thing is, I had seen inside one before and hadn't been impressed. There was something about the layout, the fittings, that niggled me. I would always find myself thinking, This is a stupid house. The neighbourhood we had driven through was nice enough, but when it came to the house itself I really couldn't be bothered to look at it properly.

There was one thing inside, however, that did catch my attention. Above the fireplace sat a picture of Culloden battlefield – the same place Andy and I had visited in the camper last year.

"Are these people Scottish?" I asked.

"Yeah, I think they are."

It was a weird little coincidence. But, as I say, it was really the only thing I looked at that day. Thank God for Andy. Back at the flat, he asked, "Well? What do you think?"

"Didn't like it."

"Did you even look at it?"

"Nah, it's a base house. Don't like em."

"Actually Joy, that was a nice house."

"Was it?"

"You never looked at it?"

"Nah."

"Right. We'll go back and see it again."

Well. We all make mistakes, I suppose. On our second viewing, I could see that Andy was right – it was a nice house. Lots of space, in good condition. I could get used to the weird features, I told myself –

things like the rooms having multiple doors. So, after all that kerfuffle, we went for it and made an offer. It was accepted.

Two Scots, buying from two other Scots – what were the chances? Of course, this also meant that we had met our match when it came to the sale. Despite our best efforts, they wouldn't budge on either the asking price or the move-in date. The timing couldn't have been better – or tighter, depending on how you look at it. We moved into the Barclay Crescent house on 8th November 2018, and our stuff arrived on Monday 11th! It was a down-to-the-wire finish, but it didn't matter! At long last, we had our own house in Alice Springs.

9

THE SWEET AND THE SOUR

(November 2018 to January 2019)

From the squalor of the little flat to... a labyrinth of boxes. Boxes everywhere. When all your stuff has found its place in your home, you forget how much of it there is. It effectively disappears. But before it's found its place, when it arrives in a new space, you're confronted by the sheer volume of it all.

Even the Pickfords guys commented on it, the cheeky sods. We were just like, "Well, this is our stuff!" Still, I won't pretend it wasn't intimidating. The mountain of boxes facing us was simply overwhelming. I really didn't want to unpack.

Gradually, though, we saw the benefits. It had been over a year since we'd last seen our stuff in Scotland. It was a wonderful feeling – a bit like being reunited with an old friend whose face you can't quite remember until they're right in front of you. All the bits and pieces we associated with our old home were finally joining us in our new one.

The furniture, in particular, was a sight for sore eyes. To see our own bed, and our comfortable leather chairs again... needless to say, it was the total opposite of the grimy flat that had held us hostage. By Monday night we were sitting in our own place, watching our own telly, surrounded by all the objects we needed to make a home.

By the time we were settled in, the Aussie summer had hit. Did I already mention the insane heat that passes as standard in Alice? When we had arrived, back in May, the temperature could reach about 23 degrees – positively balmy by Scottish standards. If you were lucky, the winter would only last about three weeks, from the start of June. But the end of November marks the start of summer, and we were now looking at the mid-30s – scorching weather! The sunshine was probably my favourite thing about Australia, full stop. I'd never gotten so much sun in my life.

From our previous trips out to see the kids, we had a good sense of how to enjoy the heat too. Throwing some shrimp on the barbie is a stereotype for good reason – barbecuing is an absolute staple of summer life in Australia. You put your tinnies or stubbies in your Esky and you head to the nearest barbie. It's a big social gathering point. Everyone brings their own booze, which is a bit different to back home. The host does supply the food though – it's their barbie after all.

With our new place sorted, we were finally able to enjoy a bit of the Aussie life we had dreamed of. Long summer afternoons basking in the hot sun, keeping ourselves topped up with food and drink, enjoying some music. Fine, we still didn't know anyone in Alice, apart from the estate agents, but maybe that could start to change now. Andy had made a few pals down at the local karate club, and I always ended up chatting to someone when I went out to walk Barney. We might not have a fully-fledged sense of community quite yet, but surely it was a matter of time.

Innis came over for Christmas. It was wonderful seeing him. We celebrated by opening our presents in 40-degree heat!

Even by Australian standards, Alice Springs is a little world of its own. It's completely different to the rest of the country – which meant that it was a new experience for us too. It was nothing like Perth or Dunsborough.

Why? Partly, it was due to the town's demographic. Alice is more Aboriginal run, so the culture and feel of the place just has a different vibe. A lot of Aboriginals live off the earth – they'd sleep out in the parks, or in the riverbed. The weather certainly allows for it, so it's not an unusual thing compared with a lot of other places, where they might call it vagrancy. It's not exactly homelessness in the way we think of it in the UK, although there are major problems with poverty in Aboriginal communities. Essentially, the people who do it seem to feel very close to nature. As one Aboriginal guy asked Andy, "Have you slept out under the stars yet?"

"No. Joy doesn't like camping."

"Oh, you don't need a tent! Just go to the park!"

It's a different mindset.

Alice is built along the Todd River, which hardly ever flows because it hardly ever rains. In a country that's largely desert, rain is a big deal. And one day, when Andy was working away, it started to rain quite heavily. I saw on the Alice Springs Facebook page, 'The Todd River is flowing!' It was really quite an event for the locals, and I wanted to see what all the fuss was about. I was imagining this tremendous rush of water, something really dramatic... I couldn't wait to see the big moment everyone was talking about.

But when I got there, it was just a big puddle.

Is that it?

Again, it's the cultural gap. In Scotland, we've got rain to spare. You get a few spots on your windscreen, and you just clear it. To the people in Alice, that would be a flood. Any amount of rain was an event; a light shower meant it was chucking it down.

"Did you see the rain last night?" someone asked later.

"Oh yeah, just a wee drizzle."

"No – that was rain all right! We haven't had that for months."

"Right."

It's all relative.

The same is true of the heat – being from Scotland, we really didn't have to think too much about what we were wearing on a given day, because it almost always felt hot to us. Conor's mum, who is from Denny in Scotland, only ever needed to wear a denim jacket during the Western Australian winter! In Alice the climate's a bit different, so you actually do feel cold during winter. I can remember one occasion when Sally, Andy's mum, called us from Nairn.

"Oh, it's a lovely day here in Nairn!"

"How hot is it?"

"About 16 degrees!"

I told her it was 19 degrees in Alice and we still needed the fire on.

"What? That's just silly!"

I had my fleece on and all.

For the locals, the changes in temperature were even more pronounced. The transition from autumn to winter on 1st June was a big thing. They'd say things to you like, "Oh wow, what a difference between today and yesterday!"

Andy and I would just look at each other covertly, thinking, There's basically no difference.

The Aboriginals had it worst – in winter they'd dress up like they were in Antarctica, walking around with big coats and hats. They'd give us a look like, "You're obviously British!"

As I've mentioned, there could be tension between the white Aussies and the Aboriginals. Those early meetings in Coles had shown me that a lot of the animosity against Aboriginals was unfair. But at the same time, racism seemed to be a part of Australian life, and its effects went deep. You couldn't ignore it.

We saw this in various ways during our time in Alice. On one occasion, Andy went out to his karate class in the evening – and came straight back again.

"Wait till I tell you this," he said.

He had been to the cash machine to get some money out for the class. As he got close, he suddenly realised he was far from alone. A group of about 12 to 14 kids was hanging around, watching him approach. The lads were young – only about eight or nine – but there were so many of them. And they knew what they were doing.

"What's wrong mister – do you want us to help you? Want us to put your PIN number in?"

It was intimidating as hell, Andy said. These kids were tiny, but he knew they would fleece him if he gave them the chance.

"Uh... I've forgotten it," he managed.

"Are you sure? Want me to try? Gimme your card."

"Nah, sorry son – can't remember it. I'm gonna have to go home."

That was it. He went off in the car, went to the karate class and explained he couldn't pay that night. When he explained what had happened, they agreed he'd done the right thing.

"Oh, they're little sods. You have to watch out for them."

On his way home he saw the same group of kids throwing stones at cars. There was really nothing to do in Alice, so they were turning into little hooligans.

But you can't generalise, and I really don't want to. Apart from that episode at the cash point, we never had any trouble with the Aboriginals. On the contrary, Andy worked with a bunch of Aboriginal guys when he was off doing his painting, and they got on really well. Again, there were cultural differences, but when you actually get to know people a bit more, those end up being more of a benefit than a problem.

With Andy's colleagues, there was a meeting of minds – they learned from each other. Every day at 10am they'd have their 'smoke-o' – a tea break. Andy would be like, "Right, I'll go and get the coffees."

They stared at him. "What do you mean, 'go and get the coffees'?"

"I'll just pop out to Hungry Jack's." That was a good place to get carry-out coffee.

"You're going to get us a coffee?"

They couldn't believe it.

"I'll tell you what – you buy it tomorrow. I'll take you in the works van."

"Yeah... OK."

It seemed like they were so used to being treated as second class citizens by white people that this idea, of taking turns to get coffee, didn't compute. It's like the inequality had become normalised. A lot of people called Aboriginals 'blackfellas' – they called themselves that too. But sometimes there's just this nasty undercurrent. We saw it with Graham, the white South African.

"Back in South Africa we just get the blackfellas to do it," he blustered.

He was prejudiced, as well as being a nasty piece of work.

Andy found some more common ground with his colleagues when he discovered they were into fishing. A couple of them were from the Torres Strait islands off the north of Australia, a father and son. They grew to like each other.

"If you ever get a break from here, we'll take you back to our home," the dad suggested. "We'll go out fishing."

"That sounds nice, I like fishing. What rods do you use?"

"Rods?"

They were spear fishers. It might seem obvious, but you really do find similarities wherever you are in the world – they just look a bit different to what you're used to.

Not even all the boxes

Andy decorating the living room

Our garden

The Todd Mall, Alice Springs

The temperature on the 7th December

The Christmas tree outside the council building in Alice Springs

10

SHOWDOWN

(January to March 2019)

It was 2019, our first new year as Aussie residents. We had been living in Australia for nearly a year and a half, though it had all been such a whirlwind we had barely had time to register it. More importantly, though, we still weren't permanent residents. Andy had been working for Harvey Developments for nearly a year, but still we were only on sponsored work visas. We had bought a house in this town, but technically we still weren't residents. It was starting to grate on me.

The main issue – the one that became the sticking point – was Andy's work. Even with the relief of getting our own place and escaping the grotty flat, and being able to have a bit more quality time together, he was still working ridiculously hard. The unfairness of the work situation had been highlighted multiple times with Peter now – but nothing had changed. Andy was still pulling these mad driving shifts out to houses in the middle of nowhere, then going straight to work on them. He'd go off on the Monday, saying he'd try to get home the next one. But in practice he wouldn't return until the next Thursday. The work trips frequently lasted about 10 or 11 days. He was running himself ragged.

A typical work trip, from Alice Springs to Tennant Creek: 508 kilometres. Or 316 miles to us Brits. About five and a half hours of driving through the sweltering heat of the red desert, with a thin scattering of places to stop along the way: Tea Tree, Wycliffe Well. If he left Alice at 7am he'd be in town by early afternoon – but sometimes later: the houses assigned to Andy were also out in the bush. Stick another three or four hours of driving on top of the first leg, heading off road in his ute (Aussie slang for a utility vehicle, or works van).

Upon arrival, a dusty and tired Andy would understandably be ready to rest. But no: it's only the afternoon, and there are a few hours of the working day left, never mind the gruelling drive. He's expected to commence work right away. When you add it all up it's a 10-hour day – and then he takes his sleeping bag and beds down in a donga (temporary housing) on site. Often this includes a kitchen that has been well used by meat eaters, with facilities uncleaned... hardly ideal for a veggie.

The whole thing was awful – and it wasn't just me who felt that way, either. When Lewis came over to see us in late April, we finally reached a tipping point. Innis and Hazel had already paid us a visit, so we had a wonderful few weeks with them. Lewis could only visit for five days, as he had a wedding to go to in Bali. Unbeknownst to us he would have to make a ridiculous trip of his own to get there, flying from Alice to Adelaide to Perth, and finally on to Bali. It just shows you how wonderful our kids are. Rather than thinking, Screw you, Mum and Dad, he really wanted to use his holiday to see us, even if it meant multiple stopovers on the return trip. It had been about a year since we had last been face-to-face, and a lot had changed since then.

Andy was away on a job when Lewis arrived, on a Saturday. There was a house viewing I wanted to go to – another of my pastimes in Alice.

"Right," I told Lewis. "The house next door is up for sale. I want to have a nosey – come with me."

Some days I'd see a few houses on the trot, in a single day. Then I'd come away thinking, *Nah – don't like any of em!*

It was at this house viewing that we met Karen, who would go on to buy the house and become one of our main contacts in Alice. She's still kind enough to keep an eye on our place, and had we lived there longer she would have become a good neighbour and a better friend.

After the viewing, Lewis and I had the whole day together. At about half one in the afternoon we cracked open a bottle of wine – it's five o'clock somewhere, as my motto goes. We drank and chatted away, catching up after a year apart. It was about half six or seven when Andy finally arrived home, looking half dead. He had been working that morning and had just driven back from God knows where.

"Look how thin your father is," I said to Lewis. The weight was dropping off him. Lewis gave his old man a hug.

"You're a bag of bones," he agreed.

We started talking about the job. The more details Andy shared, the more disgusted Lewis became.

"Dad, this is ridiculous. This wasn't the reason you came over here."

We couldn't disagree with him. But this was just how things had turned out. Andy needed that job for us to stay in Australia. It was the price we had to pay.

It was then that Andy's phone rang. Even without it being on speaker, the voice on the other end was easy to hear: It was shouting. Graham had called Andy up, furious, to take him to task. He was angry that he had left the job he was on, and had driven home instead of going straight on to the next one.

"No," Andy protested, calm but firm. "I've done my 10 days, as agreed. I'm going to spend some time at home with my son now."

The yelling on the other end intensified.

It was all out in the open now. After the call, Lewis was livid.

"I've a mind to go up to that office myself for a word, Dad. Because I do not like the way you're being spoken to."

As an Australian citizen, he may well have been in a better position to speak up than we were. But, aside from the fact that Andy can stick up for himself, we were convinced it wouldn't do any good at this stage. Things were dire enough; we had no intention of making them worse.

Finally, after some more back and forward, Lewis made another suggestion.

"You know, you should just go on the sick and get this sorted. Get the union involved. You've got to get this sorted out."

There was no way around it: the lad was right. We had both been doing our best to get on with things, but the bare facts were indisputable. This was a raw deal. Poor Andy was being ground down by this work, and Harvey Developments was a bad employer, never thinking about the needs of their people – just the bottom line. It came out in the details. They didn't pay any extra money or expenses for the travelling Andy had to do – which amounted to hours, if not days. They had the most basic facilities imaginable, and plenty of stringent rules that made things even more difficult. Andy wasn't supposed to take the ute into town – which meant he had no way to get a bite to eat after a six-hour drive. They just expected him to start working straight away. They treated their employees like slaves.

"You're working away for days," Lewis continued. "You're losing weight. This isn't right."

All of it would have been worth it if Peter had been true to his word and had gotten our permanent resident status in motion. Then we'd have the option to look for some other work. But he hadn't – at least as far as we could tell. It was like Andy was indentured to the company, because of the sponsorship. They had us right where they wanted us.

Andy phoned Peter up again, in an effort to remind him of the agreement. He was, as usual, completely blasé.

"Oh yeah, don't you worry about it! Everything's fine. Enjoy having your son over!"

Blah blah blah. Hangs up.

We had dreamt of Australia as a new life. A better life, closer to our kids and, perhaps, future grandkids. It was supposed to be our fresh start.

The problem was, we had become completely stuck. Of course, you have to make some sacrifices when you move somewhere new. But hadn't we already been through enough to get here? Hadn't we given enough? Why the hell should Andy have to slave away like this, with no end in sight? It wasn't right, and it wasn't freedom. It wasn't the life we'd dreamt of.

After the conversation with Lewis, Andy bit the bullet and went to see a doctor the following Monday. He explained how much stress he was under from work, that he was losing weight at an alarming rate. She was more than happy to sign him off sick.

Before Lewis headed off to Bali, he also put us in touch with Kane, the union man who covered the whole of the Northern Territory. Despite being remarkably busy, he did a huge amount for us in the case against Harvey Developments. He really was our saviour.

The way I saw it, Andy was never really given the chance he had been promised. He was working as a travelling tradesman, not as the manager of a department. Because of the hold Graham seemed to have on Peter, Andy never got an opportunity to shine. Graham was haemorrhaging money out of that company. He'd do 10- or 12-hour drives up to Darwin for no apparent reason. He couldn't work the tools like Andy could – he was a useless manager, frankly.

Jenny, Peter's wife, had told me they planned to get rid of him. But what did that have to do with Andy? Why was he a threat to Graham? In fact, had Peter realised what was going on, he also might have realised that Andy could have helped him run the company better. He could have made him more money.

It's funny how these things come to a head. For the first half of

2019, with no glimmer of our permanent residencies in sight, I stewed on the unfairness of our situation. I was restless, sat at home waiting for Andy to return from his latest stint.

We spoke later that day. It was then that I learned that Andy was doing yet more house cleaning, rather than painting and decorating. In fact, he was way out in the bush, scrubbing away at some particularly grotty Aboriginal houses.

It was too much. In a heartbeat, I saw red.

I drove to the office. In truth, I think they were always a bit frightened of me, because I wouldn't let them off the hook. I'd tried my best to be measured over the last six months, but my God I was *angry* with the lot of them that day. I marched into the office.

"Where's Peter?" I asked Emily, the secretary.

"Oh Miss Joy, Miss Joy, you can't..."

Shut up you stupid woman.

Clearly they did not want me in there. But Peter soon emerged. This wasn't the first time I had invaded their office to give them a good jarring. It was the least they deserved, with the situation they were putting us in.

"Do you know where Andrew is working right now?" I said to Peter.

He turned to the secretary. "Ah Emily, where's Andrew–"

"You don't need to ask Emily. I'll tell ya."

I was really pissed off now. I wanted him to admit what was going on.

"You've sent him five and a half hours away to clean Aboriginal houses. He's cleaning them. Houses that are running with cockroaches! He's a tradesman, and you've got him doing that!"

I wasn't going to let him dodge the bullet this time. It was time for a proper showdown.

Peter glared at me. Muscles tensed, he slammed his laptop shut, pushed it towards me and said, "You know what? He can leave."

Game on, pal.

"I'll tell you what – he's not leaving. Because you have gotten us here. You got us the sponsorship. We have bought a house here because you said you'd help us with our PRs." I fixed him with my best death stare. "We're going nowhere."

Peter doesn't like confrontation. He looked furious, and I could only imagine what he was thinking, something along the lines of: *Oh, this little shit of a woman has marched in here and put me in my place!*

Annoying Emily broke the silence: "Oh Mrs Joy, Mrs Joy, Mr Peter does not need this."

"Emily, this has got nothing to do with you!"

But on she went. Peter let her stand there, and I just ignored the little bitch. I wanted to give her a Glasgow kiss.

At last, Peter showed his hand.

"Graham's not going anywhere," he says.

"I don't *care* about Graham! I am here because you've sent my husband all those miles away to work in Aboriginal houses that are *filthy*. Because you're expecting him to clean them before he decorates them!"

Then he started to question the quality of Andy's work! Saying he hadn't painted the tops of the doors, for God's sake!

"Look Peter, I don't wanna hear it! I know what a good worker Andy is – I can't believe you're even criticising his work!"

"I don't care what you think, Joy!"

Now he was getting aggressive. But I wouldn't let him off the hook – not this time. We had been waiting for months on end for the security this man had promised, and had he delivered? He was, as we say in Scotland, an empty shite! How could I respect someone who had sold us a pack of lies?

It was too late now, anyway. It had all come out in one big eruption – no more polite dodges. I had made my point, and they were just itching to chuck me out of that office. They didn't have to wait much longer. I had said my piece.

"I'm going, I've wasted your time as it is."

I put my hand out to shake his, and to his credit, he took it.

He said, "Don't worry Joy, you're OK. Everything will be all right."

Lying shit.

I got in the car and I cried all the way back to my house with the *rage*.

They're just treating us like second-class citizens. They don't respect us; because we're Scottish they think we know nothing. That we just live off haggis...

I came back to Barney. He looked up at me with those big, doleful eyes.

At least he would give me a proper hearing. I said, "Wait till I tell you this..."

Poor Barney. He must have been thinking, *Gosh. Here we go again!*

The thing is, by the time the showdown happened I already knew there was no way we were getting those permanent residencies out of Peter. I sometimes get these instincts with things, and I've learned to trust them. Sure, perhaps the conversation could have gone differently. But Andy and I had both had enough of the whole situation – it was a matter of time before the truth came out.

I phoned Andy after the showdown, to fill him in on the latest.

"Look, this is what happened. It probably wasn't the right thing, but now it's done..."

We had lived in that grotty flat for over six months to save money, but even though we had escaped it, nothing else had changed. We were still completely beholden to the company, who had lied to us, who wouldn't give us our due. In truth all that anger had been brewing for quite some time. It had just needed its moment.

11

EXIT STRATEGY

(August to October 2019)

How did it all unravel so quickly? It seemed like only yesterday we had arrived in Alice, ready to start a new chapter of our lives. But just nine months later, in August 2019, Andy quit his job at Harvey Developments. It had been months in the making; he had been on the sick since February, and after the confrontation in May there was no turning back.

After the blow-out happened, I invited Jenny, Peter's wife, round for a coffee. I wanted to get a handle on the damage. Out of all the people involved with the company, Jenny was by far the most reasonable. I had been able to speak honestly with her before about the condition of the flat, and when we met up in town I asked her if she was aware of the confrontation in the office.

"Yes, Peter told me about it. But why didn't you come to me first, Joy?"

"Because I think Peter needs to know how I feel, as well as Andy," I explained. "He promised he'd help us with our PRs, but we're still waiting."

I was under the impression that Jenny understood our situation. Maybe I had assumed too much.

"Oh, what's a PR?" she asked casually.

What's a PR?

I was stunned. Here I was, a transplanted Scot smack in the middle of Australia, about to explain the country's immigration system to one of its own citizens! These people didn't have a clue. They were working up in that office every day, but had they actually done any PRs for any of their employees?

Jenny reassured me that she would speak to Peter about it, and that she would come round to see me later in the week. In actual fact, I never saw her again. She sent a text explaining that she had to go to Adelaide – if that's a euphemism for disappearing off the face of the planet it's news to me. She certainly didn't indicate anything of the sort. On the contrary, she texted me a few more times making loads of suggestions for things we could do together: go swimming, join a local women's group. It all sounded wonderful, but none of it materialised. It was genuinely quite disappointing, as we seemed to be getting on quite well. But I guess it was impossible to separate the chance of a friendship from the deteriorating work situation.

In the run up to Andy quitting, we worked closely with Kane, the union organiser for the whole of the Northern Territory. He really did do all he could for us, despite his own workload being huge. We detailed all the various malpractice and unethical standards Andy had experienced during his time with Harvey Developments.

It was a strange and uncomfortable position to be in. For several months we were in limbo, completely unsure of how things would pan out.

Unknown to me, Andy had been making inquiries of his own. One day, he told me that he had applied for a job back in Inverness.

"All right then," I said. "What's the story?"

"Well... I've got an interview."

I couldn't believe it – this was nine months into Alice Springs, into our house, and Andy had an interview for a job back in Scotland. My instincts kicked in; I knew as soon as he mentioned it that he would get that job.

We were probably in slightly different headspaces by this point, too. Despite all the turmoil and disappointment, I still didn't want to leave Alice. I had dug my heels in, and was determined to make it work come Hell or high water. From Andy's point of view, it was time to start looking at other options.

He had the interview on a Thursday night. On the Friday morning he woke up to a text from the employer saying that everything had gone fine, and that they just needed to talk to him about a few things. They would call him that evening.

"Andy, they're going to offer you the job. Please don't accept it. Please tell them you need to discuss it with your family over the weekend."

"Of course I won't accept it right away. I probably won't get the job anyway."

"You will. Why would they contact you on a Friday like that if you hadn't got the job?"

"We'll have to wait and see, Joy."

"No way am I going back to Inverness! No way!"

Fast forward a few hours, and the employer is calling. Andy puts them on loudspeaker.

Just bloody say it then.

A voice crackled over the speaker.

"Well, basically Andrew, we want to offer you the job."

That was it. Straight away I started crying. I had to retreat to the bedroom. When I resurfaced, I learned that Andy had been given until Monday to decide whether he would take the job.

We called the kids. They couldn't believe what we were suggesting.

"But you've spent so much money just to get out here! You can't do it!"

Of course, that was exactly how I felt. I was really bucking against the whole idea. But the writing was on the wall. We had the weekend to mull it over, but when you know, you know. By the Monday, even though I was coming round to the possibility of returning to Scotland, I was also clinging onto the hope that something else would happen. That a new job would drop out of the sky, or some equivalent miracle. It didn't materialise. The fact was, the job offer back home was the miracle. It was our ticket out of this whole debacle with Harvey Developments.

Andy called the employer back that evening and accepted the job. Then he quit the Harvey Developments gig, and our sponsorship was officially up in smoke, along with any possibility of being granted the fabled permanent residency visas. Without work, our temporary visas started counting down. We had 60 days to get out.

It had been a tough decision, but it also felt like the right one. We had fought long and hard to adapt to Australia and Alice – to fit into the way of life here as outsiders. To some extent we had succeeded. It's important to separate the dispute with the company from Alice Springs itself, because we had grown to love the place. But feeling connected to somewhere doesn't count for much when your quality of life is low. Andy had lost a tonne of weight from the work, and was only just recovering. I was sick to death of how he was being treated, and the fact he was away so much. We had both just had enough, and the dream we had been pushing towards for years suddenly seemed more like a nightmare that we needed to escape from.

So we faced facts, and started making our exit strategy. It seemed like only yesterday that our stuff had arrived, shipped over from Scotland. Now it was time to repack and ship out. This time we made a concerted effort to get rid of things we didn't need; we had learned our lesson from the last mountain of boxes, and we were ruthless. We took enough stuff to the thrift store to fill the place up.

Goodbyes were said to the few friends we had made: Sam the estate agent, Karen, our new neighbour, and Kane, our union connection.

Then, one day, it was time to get in the car and go. It was a sad moment. As we shut the gate of our house and pulled away, it really felt like we were leaving something important behind.

"It's just so sad it's come to an end," I said to Andy as we drove towards the edge of town, the low houses and yards retreating behind us.

"Well, what else can we do?" he reflected. "This is probably the best thing."

Indeed, we had talked it over in enough detail to know that it was. Still, I couldn't pretend it didn't sting.

"We can come back though, can't we?"

"I don't see why anything would stop us."

And that was the whole point, really, wasn't it? Despite all our reservations, and all the obstacles in our way, we had made a serious go of a new life in an unfamiliar place. A place where the sun always seemed to be shining, where the culture was strange yet not altogether alien, where we had been the fresh faces.

We had lived there, and we had accepted it. It wasn't like when the Brits go abroad and have to have English food and football. We had proven to ourselves that we could find out feet in the unknown, and with that knowledge came the sense that, if we really wanted to, we could also do it all over again. Nothing could stop us. At the very least, we'd certainly be going back for future holidays.

Although it all went horribly wrong, we felt no bitterness towards Alice Springs. We still don't, because we simply loved living there. We might be leaving for now, but that couldn't eclipse the fact that we now had a deeper connection with Australia than ever before. The door we had opened hadn't closed; it stood ajar. It still does.

Me and my girl!

Andy and I

Andy and I

EPILOGUE

The Return Home

For reasons unknown, the journey back over the Nullarbor was quicker: we managed it in just five days. Maybe it was because we were truly ready to leave: there was no time for messing about. The roadhouses and dead kangaroos swept by in a blur. Before we knew it, we were back in Perth for one last week at Hazel and Conor's.

We had come out to Australia all together, but we would be returning one by one. Because of his job, Andy needed to head back pronto, so he flew home first, followed by Barney. Finally, it was my turn... and it was just awful. I thought I had made my peace with leaving, but it wasn't quite that simple. As the day of my flight loomed closer and closer, I was filled with dread. I didn't want to fly alone. But, even stronger than that, I didn't want to leave.

It was Hazel who got me over the fear. Maybe it was the last little push I needed. She understood exactly what was going on.

"When I flew back on my own for Granny's funeral, I was terrified," she told me. "Conor dropped me off at the airport and I just thought, What am I doing?"

Which was just how I felt. The future, the return flight to Scotland, was stretched out before me, utterly forbidding.

"Mum, you can do this," Hazel continued. "You don't need Dad's hand. You can do it yourself. You're stronger than you think."

She was right – I just didn't know it yet. It was like I had to prove to myself that, after everything we had been through, I could still get on that plane and leave Australia. My wee heart was breaking, but I had to do it.

So that's exactly what I did.

As I've mentioned, I always had a sense of a parallel between Alice Springs and Nairn, both being small towns. Perhaps that's why, on our arrival home, Andy and I bought a house in Nairn. It was like we had brought the memory of Alice back with us to the Highlands.

We had left the familiarity of Scotland behind for the unknown, for adventure – and, even with that funny echo between Alice and Nairn, that was the thing I really missed now. The wildness of Australia. When you live in a seaside town, you're stuck with frigging seagulls... not quite as exciting as the bright little parrots you'd see in Alice. The lovely, dusty red dingoes, deadly but beautiful. The roos and emus, of course. I'd think back to the time when Hazel and I were driving down to see Lewis and were confronted by an emu crossing the road! It was unreal. There was the bad stuff too of course: cockroaches, cicada and snakes, my worst nightmare.

It summed up the whole experience, really. Our Aussie adventure had had its highs and lows, its good and bad moments. One thing it never was was boring. It had been one of the brightest, most colourful chapters of our lives.

At the start of 2020, back in Nairn and before the COVID-19 pandemic hit, I shared an epic Facebook post. I laid it all out, line by line – the decision to move to Australia, the journey out, the months spent in Perth and Dunsborough, the gruelling drive to Alice, our life in the red centre...

After it was done, I stared at it in a state of disbelief. Had Andy and I really done all this stuff? It seemed unreal, but we had.

At the start of the post I had written something that grabbed me.

'I could write a book.'

Hey... that's not a bad idea, you know.

AN AUSSIE/SCOTTISH DICTIONARY

For those who need a little help with the local dialogue – on either side!

Donga (Aussie) – A portable, temporary living space. Often found at building sites.

Esky (Aussie) – A portable mini fridge. Ideal for transporting your tinnies to a barbie.

Glasgow Kiss (Scottish) – A specifically Scotch greeting that's also likely to be a goodbye!

Oner (Scottish) – A single long journey, done in one go.

Servo (Aussie) – A service station. Vital when on the road to Alice Springs.

Ute (Aussie) – A utility vehicle.

Printed in Great Britain
by Amazon

54419466R00070